WHEN CULTURES COLLIDE
ADULT MISSIONARY KIDS

WHEN CULTURES COLLIDE

ADULT MISSIONARY KIDS

Edie Bakker

Scriptures, unless otherwise specified, are quoted are from the *GOOD NEWS BIBLE* © 1994 published by the Bible Societies/Harper Collins Publishers Ltd UK, Good News Bible© American Bible Society 1966, 1971, 1976, 1992. Used with permission. All rights reserved.

Verses marked KJV are taken from the King James Version of the Holy Bible.

These two versions were popular on the mission field in the 1970s and 1980s.

Scriptures marked NKJV are taken from the *NEW KING JAMES VERSION* (NKJV): Scripture taken from the *NEW KING JAMES VERSION*®. Copyright© 1982 by Thomas Nelson, Inc. Used by permission. All rights reserved.

Scriptures marked TLB are taken from the *THE LIVING BIBLE* (TLB): Scripture taken from *THE LIVING BIBLE* copyright© 1971. Used by permission of Tyndale House Publishers, Inc., Carol Stream, Illinois 60188. All rights reserved.

Scriptures marked NLT are taken from the *HOLY BIBLE, NEW LIVING TRANSLATION* (NLT): Scriptures taken from the *HOLY BIBLE, NEW LIVING TRANSLATION*, Copyright© 1996, 2004, 2007 by Tyndale House Foundation. Used by permission of Tyndale House Publishers, Inc., Carol Stream, Illinois 60188. All rights reserved. Used by permission.

Scriptures marked NIV are taken from the *NEW INTERNATIONAL VERSION* (NIV): Scripture taken from *THE HOLY BIBLE, NEW INTERNATIONAL VERSION*®. Copyright© 1973, 1978, 1984, 2011 by Biblica, Inc.™. Used by permission of Zondervan

ISBN 13: 978-0-9882175-4-6
ISBN 10: 0-9882175-4-6

Published by Shiloh House Books
1340 Travis Lane
Kaufman TX 75142

Cover design: Janet Long
Photos on Cover are with permission from Jamey Dye.

Contact: Edie Bakker at: edierainforest@yahoo.com

DEDICATION

This book is dedicated to Missionary Kids everywhere who have somehow survived the challenge of suddenly having to change their beliefs, culture and lifestyle.

This book is also written with deep appreciation for my children, Gabriel and Sarah, who put up with the time I put into it during their formative years.

ACKNOWLEDGMENTS

Many thanks go to Sue Mortimer and Linda Sudyk for their help with the specific cultural ethics and values listed in this book. Sue was raised in Mexico and Linda was raised in the United States. They each spent years coaching me, guiding me, and collaborating with me on this book.

Also thanks to Rob Bakker and Janet Long

Although I do have a bachelor's degree in Anthropology, the data for this book came from the hard-earned experience of myself and my many MK friends and not from tables and surveys. For some this will lessen the book's value. For others it will increase it.

OUTLINE

Biblical principles for choosing the values that are right for you in the culture in which you are called to live!

Discusses the way values become intertwined so that one cannot be changed without affecting another. Also discusses the absence of hidden skills required to conform to certain values.

Talks about the Spiritual implications in the lives of those who find themselves unable to do what they think is right. God's unconditional love.

A fun look at what Americans may look like to people from another land.

The maturity of MKs
East, West, People and Things
Mixing Conversations
Marrying Internationally
Making a good impression

Presents the problems of "Child Abuse" on the field, prejudices, demonic oppression brought on by exposure to cults on the field, physical illness caused by being raised on the field and emotional illness.

*A **chart** for predicting MK possible struggles*

1

"MKs"

I SHUFFLED MY bare feet under the wooden desk and stared out the window between the glass louvers at the distant pink hills. It was my favorite season, when the air was cool and dry, and the grass on the hills threw up their long, seeded pink stems and softly colored the horizon. Clouds shifted lazily by, covering a sky of cobalt blue. From behind the trees at the end of the school playing field, came the tapping, sawing, and grinding sounds of the men at work in the shop and sawmill. A gentle breeze ruffled the thin fir trees just outside the school window. In only another hour, the bell would ring, and I could be off, riding my Honda bike past those shops, across the old iron bridge, over the winding dirt road and up into those very hills. I tried to pull my mind back to the matter at hand.

"My life as a deprived missionary kid!" was the title of the essay our teacher had asked us to write, in deference to the wishes of the mission's home branch. Sullen resentment disturbed my usually creative mind as I searched for a way to disprove the assumptions behind the title. I closed my eyes and in a moment, I was floating down a crystal clear jungle stream, my head resting gently on the warm wooden prow of our dug-out canoe, as I listened lazily to the parrots in the tops of the trees above. In the U.S. I could have been watching TV. How had they dared even to pose such a question?

"Perhaps," I thought, "I could tell them about being the very first explorers into uncharted areas of the jungle, discovering exotic waterfalls and capturing rare animals. Or maybe they would rather hear about traveling around the world to Europe, the Philippines, and Japan, in addition to our home in Papua New Guinea. Maybe I should tell them about flying low over the jungle in an open helicopter on a survey, or discovering new caves, or snorkeling and collecting on beaches strewn with fresh shells."

How could I begin to write a story which illustrated the fullness and depth of the life I had always loved. The life I had come to feel was the ultimate and only true life. It seemed, on furloughs in the U.S., that all there was to do was to dream about, and watch movies of the life I now lived! Even in everyday things, there was more adventure and more flavor to what we did than what we heard of others doing. Every summer we lived off of wild game and fish. I helped mom deliver babies, and the boys helped dad run the boats. We swam every night, made up a little vacation bible school for a whole crowd of half-naked children, and paddled our own canoes into glamorous tropical sunsets. The center where we attended school was symbolically covered with flowers all year around. All of the adults were Christians and we were free to go wherever and whenever we wished. We climbed tall smooth gum trees, slept out under the stars on Friday nights, ate fruit from lush tropical gardens and played as if the entire center was one exotic private backyard.

When we reached our teens, we had more friends than most American kids can imagine. I can remember feeling lonely and "deprived" if I ever had so much as one thought that I couldn't immediately share with someone around me who loved me deeply. I can't ever remember having to be alone at the mission base or center.

Most MKs, or missionaries' kids, would rather call their childhood "paradise" than "deprivation". Few would say that they regret having grown up overseas. Of course, there are some really terrible things that happen to some kids overseas, such as insensitive boarding schools, war, and illness. But on the whole, most of us accepted those tragedies as part of life—part of a good life.

So what is all this talk of "deprived MKs"? And why do many MKs have "problems" as adults? That partly depends on how you define "problems". Many people concerned about adult MKs are looking into the MK's childhood, trying to identify things which would cause the MK to have emotional problems as an adult. They are finding some things. So as not to overlook those things, in chapter 11 of this book I have included a discussion of some negative childhood circumstances which have affected some MK adults. However, this book is not about those things. It is about something far more prevalent and insidious and quite universal to Adult MKs.

The majority of MKs were given a wonderful childhood, and at 18, were marvelously mature and healthy adults. It is the loss of their culture, and their reluctance to take on a new, seemingly inferior culture, which causes so much stress for adult MKs. Indeed, so much stress that many are over-whelmed and virtually all have more adjustment problems than they themselves expected or would care to admit. While some MKs are able to use their wonderful childhood experi-ences to their advantage, and go farther in society than most people, many others are caught in a devastating cycle of what seems to them to be depressing failure. They are unable to re-solve the hundreds of cultural conflicts which they encounter every day. The ethics and values which they have been raised to firmly believe in simply do not agree with those of the so-ciety where they are expected to spend their entire adult life.

In 1978, I packed a suitcase, said good-bye to my family, and moved to the U.S. "for good". That day was the end of my first life and the beginning of my second.

· · · · ·

In the United States:

"Just wait until the light turns green and then go for it," Johnny said.

I tried to stop my 10-speed bicycle with the hand brakes, but I pulled the wrong one and lurched forward. This was more bike and way more traffic than I was used to. We were actually in the same lane as the speeding cars!

"Can't you stay out of the way!" another teen exclaimed. The light turned, and the rest of the teenagers' bikes raced ahead on the harrowing journey from church to Julie's house where the pizza party was about to start. It was a sports party and my Great Aunt Margaret, whom I rented a room from, thought getting to know the teens at our youth group was a good idea.

I didn't know anything about football and didn't understand the point of two sides ramming into each other over a ball that couldn't even bounce straight. I sat off to the side and wondered what to say, but no one talked to me. Finally, the pizza arrived, and someone set about collecting the money to pay for it.

"You got five dollars? I was asked.

"No, I don't have any money," I replied sheepishly, wondering what to do and why no one had said to bring money. If they had I probably wouldn't have come because I could make food cheaper at home.

"Do you have enough money to cover for me?" I asked. I was used to people sharing. They shared, but gathered around me.

"She won't pay her share!" one kid announced. I wanted to crawl into a hole.

"That's BOLD!" another girl proclaimed, tossing back her hair. It was obvious "bold" did not mean "brave," it meant something like "rude and stupid."

"Please ride with me home," I asked Johnny who had come along as a chaperon.

I went to one more party. Amazingly I played 8-ball at the very beginning and shot all the balls in, in the right order, with one shot! It was a break from the Lord, I decided, since after that the other teens showed a little more respect. But we still had nothing in common. I didn't dare to play another game of 8-ball since winning had only been a fluke.

One of the boys at that party took me out later to a restaurant, just the two of us. I never thought of it as a date. After all, I was engaged. But how else could I make a friend? We had a good conversation and somewhere towards the end I casually mentioned, "I love you." This was how we all ended our conversations on the mission field and I meant nothing more than love in the Lord. But he took it differently and soon began "harassing" me with phone calls and suggested marriage. I was shocked and couldn't understand.

My issues with the youth group were over because I never went back but my trials with the U.S. had just begun. I tried talking to older people in my church, but they were quickly turned off as I was not used to casual conversation and would immediately share my deepest thoughts. I was told I wore my heart on my sleeve. I also purposely put myself down. It was how we talked where I grew up but for some reason it only made people look down on me.

Little did I know that this was more than culture shock and I was not just bad at communicating. We were conflicting in ways I could not and would not change because my whole belief system differed drastically from theirs.

I found love in my Grandma Edith's care. She had had MKs live with her in her home many years before. I had her friendship, and that of my Aunt Margaret, but even there, there were serious issues.

I was ecstatic when the first snowflakes fell in late September after school started at my community college. I had no idea how cold it would soon be. The dark clouds of Michigan were impenetrable and soon I needed a very warm coat. My fiancé, Rob, who was also a missionary kid and lived in Texas, brought me a feather army jacket, but it was not good enough for my aunt. "I will not be seen with you at church in such an ugly thing!" she declared. "You need something that is in style. That's why people don't like you!" She took me to a department store where the coats were long and heavy and looked like blankets with few buttons. She insisted that one of these was perfect for me and that I must put it in layaway. It would cost more than a month's rent. Later I cringed when she announced that we could not afford a Christmas tree even though there was a farm down the road that sold them for just $10. This was said at a restaurant where our dinner cost $35.

I felt deeply guilty about that coat. I was borrowing money I didn't have and worse yet, I was spending the Lord's money on something that did not seem to be a real need. Both actions seemed wrong to me, but so did disobeying my aunt and she probably had a better idea about why people didn't like me than I did. I had always had about 20 friends at home and now I had none. It put me in a double bind. I would feel guilty no matter what I did. This was only one of a host of conflicts of conscience that I began to collect.

The obvious solution to this one was that I find work. I

didn't think of working at a restaurant. I hardly even knew how to order food. More importantly, I knew I had to do something for the Lord. I put the word out, hoping to find something more useful. I did. A babysitting job for a child who was very, very mentally disabled. He was challenged intellectually by folding and unfolding a lawn chair for hours and I was bored. Distracting him was impossible and I was tired of listening to his only rock music tape over and over again so while I kept a close eye on him I began to clean the house. It was badly in need of cleaning and straightening so each time I babysat I also cleaned.

Why not clean their rooms out as well? I thought, looking at their piled-high belongings. I folded and sorted and put away until I even got into their closets. That was when the problem arose. I found a note in the older brother's closet, a child not left in my care. The note mentioned his plans to make out with another girl in his elementary school and I thought I should show it to his parents. Of course, for them this was the last straw and I was fired. More shame. I had never been fired in my life.

I knew of nothing that I could do better than babysit so I gave up on working. There were so many other things I failed at or didn't understand that my sense of shame and guilt compounded.

I was also desperately lonely. We had no cell phones in those days and calls to anywhere outside of town were expensive. Calls to my fiancé were <u>very</u> expensive. Calls to my parents in Papua New Guinea were out of the question. But one night I did receive a call from them at 1:00 am in the morning. To my shock and horror, I learned that daddy had almost died months earlier with a burst appendix as he had walked out of the jungle to a rickety jeep that carried him to a native hospital. It hit me hard that they were really completely out of reach.

These days most adult missionary kids have some phone contact with their parents and friends, but they are still usually very far away. For me they were suddenly gone completely, as if dead.

I was unusual, however, in that I was the first MK to get engaged to another MK from my home school and plan a future together as soon as we got through college. One day I came home from school and found him standing in my bedroom. I had not expected him and at the sight of him I fainted. Concerned about me, he had driven 19 hours straight through on a weekend to come and surprise me.

Rob and my Grandma Edith were the tiny rocks I clung to, although usually it was just Grandma Edith. She took me everywhere and I got to know some of her friends. Her friend, Sara, a friend from Bible Study, heard that I was having trouble getting along with my aunt who often laughed at my "backwardness." Sara invited me to hang out alone at her house every Wednesday while she and the ladies met at church. I would turn on *Little House on the Prairie* and sob my eyes out at the loss of my life which had been just like it. I had been raised primarily in a little town of Christian missionaries isolated in the countryside. In our tiny school, everybody related like family to everybody else. Flowers and trees were everywhere. I missed everything about it terribly.

I carefully tended to my now only touch with nature, a few plants my aunt had bought me and two goldfish.

Part of the problem between me and my aunt was that I didn't know how to properly clean up after myself or do my share of housework. I left drops on the counters and did not dry the shower or notice dirt on the floor. We had always had a maid.

For a year I had chest pains and severe diarrhea but did not have the money to learn what was wrong. When I got my driver's license and a car, I drove to downtown Detroit to see a specialist at a big hospital. I didn't even know how to use the elevator! The whole experience was horrible, and I will pass on that description, but the doctor never discovered the cause of my illness. My mother finally mailed me pills for a parasite that was going around on the field. It had already reached my liver, as it was known to do, and affected me for several years.

There were so many things that went wrong that if I didn't have a vivid vision of hell and believe then that killing myself would put me there, I would have done it. I was drenched with guilt over things I didn't know were wrong, desperately lonely, confused, and dysfunctional in every way. I had lost my old life as an MK and been re-birthed into a new and miserable life as a total failure. Sick, depressed, and completely unable to cope.

My secular school was my escape and I finished my associate degree in a year and a half, got married and moved to Texas. From there Rob and I moved to Holland, where he was from, so he could get a green card and return to the

U.S. In Holland I was a foreigner, not "an MK" and it was not demanded that I live in any particular way. What a relief! I could finally be myself! After six months we moved from there to California and made friends at a small country church. My family had returned from Papua New Guinea, so my parents could get degrees at Fuller Seminary, two hours away and we kept in touch with grandma by phone.

After our first baby, we tried to go to the mission field. We were turned down because I believed that sending MKs back to the U.S. alone when they turned 18 was too difficult for them. I was told I was making trouble. We were later invited back to Texas to attempt to start a ranch for returning MKs. I wrote a paper on the subject, which I was invited to present at a large international conference on adult missionary kids in Ecuador. From that presentation came this book.

2

Understanding MKs:
Why Their Actions
Sometimes Don't Fit

SOMETIMES THE BEHAVIOR of Adult MKs appears socially unacceptable or inappropriate in the United States. What is not always noticed is that much of this behavior may be perfectly acceptable and even admired or respected in a missionary kid's subculture on the field where he was raised. The same action which is considered normal overseas may, in the U.S. culture, appear irresponsible, immature, offensive, or emotionally unstable.

Examples throughout this book pertain to specific situations. They don't necessarily represent the majority because MK experiences, personality, and training vary so much that it is impossible to even consider using one example to describe all MKs. However, the principles in the book are true between any two people whose culture is slightly different from each other. The culture of MKs coming back from the field is different from the culture of those who have grown up in the U.S., whatever particular culture it is, and regardless of how they choose to react to it.

The culture in the U.S. in this book refers primarily to western evangelical culture such as still exists in Christian colleges, mainstream churches and Bible belt areas. Those MKs who come back to other cultures in the U.S. may have slightly different or other issues. However, most U.S. culture, even where it has changed, is still originally based on the values and ethics of those environments.

Many times, wrong conclusions are made in counseling MKs because of the inability of the counselor to comprehend an MK's inappropriate actions as being based on his different ethics, rather than being psychological problems. **Ethics** are defined in Webster's dictionary as "beliefs which deal with good and evil or **moral** duty and practice; i.e. his only moral alternative". (**Values**, by contrast, are things a person "prizes, esteems and rates highly; i.e. things he believes to be a better alternative".) Most people are familiar with their own particular culture and are accustomed to looking for particular causes of certain behaviors. Counselors are trained to look for personal conflicts which may be causing a person to act inappropriately. When the person is of a different culture, however, his actions may not be the result of psychological conflict at all. They may, in fact, be perfectly acceptable—if not the only moral alternative—in the view of someone with his background.

To try to find a reason behind the culturally different MK's behavior, other than good conscience or belief, can compound his problem of adjustment drastically by causing the MK to think he is sinning when he is really doing what he believes is right. This is a major source of false guilt for the MK. If he listens to the advice that his behavior is wrong, he will feel guilty no matter what he does. This is because what is right in the new culture is wrong in his mind and what is right in his own culture (in his mind and conscience), now becomes also wrong! When this situation is repeated often enough, it may lead him to feel that he cannot do anything right. In addition to the obvious drastic effect this will have on his self esteem, the feeling of not ever being able to do what is right is for many people a first step away from faith in God.

A person's ethics (more so than values) may be very deep and difficult to change. In addition to being directly tied to his sense of morality, they are usually hidden in his subconscious. For example, most Americans, when asked, would not be able to say why they think it is important to work hard for one's pay even when one can receive enough money to live on by other legal means (such as welfare or grants). Yet this work ethic is so deeply ingrained in them that to purposely do otherwise would be a serious breach of conscience. To choose to leave work and live on welfare, most Americans would probably need to reassess why they believe that they should work for their money and why they could or should change that belief, before they could do so in good conscience. The MK is in that same position when he must try to live differently than the way he believes in order to live appropriately in the new culture of which he will be a part for the rest of his life. For an MK the problem is compounded by the fact that his subculture is not just any culture, but it is (his perception of) missionary subculture so therefore he is even more convinced than most that his ideas are the closest to gospel truth.

Here are some examples of misunderstood behavior based on different MK ethics and values. The following hypothetical situations are created from real-life incidents and are described as they would most likely appear to someone from American society:

Example A

Jim is a 20 year old in his second year of college after returning to the United States at 18. He is about to lose his fourth job because of his habit of continually skipping days or parts of days on the job, during which he usually spends time with his friends, particularly with his girlfriend Nancy ,with whom he does not even claim to be serious.

Jim's parents and/or a counselor's (incorrect) conclusions might be:

(1) Jim is not interested in his job and has been unable to really find his true interests and settle down.

(2) Because of a very low self esteem, (possibly due to various reasons such as children's homes or absence of parents) he is seeking love from his friends and girlfriend to the extent that he is neglecting his other responsibilities.

(3) He is lazy and is "leading Nancy on", living a carefree and irresponsible life. ("Teenage rebellion" or "the

generation gap")

(4) He is bitter at his parents for having left him and is therefore subconsciously retaliating by being careless about his responsibilities.

(5) He was just never given enough experience at a regular job (on the field) and so does not know what is expected of him.

(6) He has always had money given to him and so does not comprehend having to work for it now.

Many of these conclusions are logical and could sometimes be true. In Jim's case, however, as in many MK cases, the reason behind his behavior is a common MK ethic. Jim is acting according to his deep convictions and to act differently at this point would cause much guilt and confusion.

MK ETHIC - People's needs always come before work! Never neglect a need in a relationship for the sake of material gain or secular responsibilities. While work is important, it is not usually as important as the needs of friends.

EXPLANATION - This ideology carried to Jim's extent may seem ridiculous from an American cultural point of view, but consider the following:

(a) As Jim grew up observing his parents, he watched them regularly and consistently interrupt important translation WORK because a friend (villager) needed to buy a mosquito net for his new baby, wanted advice about selling his coffee, or asked them to come to a party (cultural feast). The work was gladly set aside for this aspect of "ministry" which in Jim's eyes

[26]

was only meeting the needs of one's friends.

(b) The people among whom Jim's parents worked very likely believed relationships should come before work, since almost all tribal peoples do.

(c) Jim's understanding was then solidified by the talk of grown ups and Sunday sermons on the importance of relating to people this way and its effect in spreading the Gospel.

(d) Jim's belief was further solidified by his understanding of Scripture because those verses which stood out to him were those which made the most sense from his cultural view.

For example:

1. Mark 14:3 9 The story of Mary anointing Jesus' feet with perfume. She wasted a lot of money (work earnings) for the sake of a relationship with Him, much to His praise and approval.

2. Luke 10:38 42 Mary spent time with Jesus and guests, and attained Jesus' admiration, while Martha was rebuked for focusing on her work in the kitchen, showing that it was slightly less important.

3. The Sermon on the Mount lists important aspects of Christianity, all of which deal with relationships, not self provision, and even denote that this is the real way to have your needs met.

4. There is the example of Jesus himself who spent his time ministering to and relating with others continually, and said, "... *The foxes have holes and the birds of the air have nests; but the Son of Man has nowhere to lay his head.*" Matthew 8:20 NKJV

5. The Bible also says that part of the greatest command-

ments is to "... *love thy neighbor as thyself*" Matthew 22:39 KJV, and that "... *the love of money is the root of all evil.*" I Timothy 6:10 KJV. This also gives a certain perspective on the relative value of work vs. relationships.

It could be especially difficult to see that Jim's behavior is primarily motivated by his conscience if any or all of the following situations occur: a) Jim himself may not have any idea why he believes it is more important to meet his friends' needs than to remain at work every day, and b) Jim may not be a very spiritually-oriented person so it may be difficult to imagine that he might be basing his actions on something that he believes is morally right, and c) Jim may indeed have problems in his life (perhaps even some of those listed earlier) which may cause him to behave inappropriately even from his own cultural point of view.

To add to the confusion, there would usually be several areas at once where Jim's different values or ethics are causing him to do various inappropriate behaviors. He may be thus exhibiting a whole range of inappropriate behavior at once, giving the illusion that his problems are quite severe. All of these things could make it extremely difficult to see that Jim's behavior may be basically the result of a very deep and not easily changeable conviction as to what he sees as right and wrong.

Example B

Mary is an 18-year-old MK in her first year of college. She seldom dresses up and is mostly seen in jeans. She has never had a real haircut (just trim). Her face is never made up and she does not wash her hair frequently (i.e., it occasionally appears oily.)

Her American friends might conclude:

1. Mary doesn't care about herself at all and is suffering from low self esteem.
2. Mary has not been taught how to take proper care of herself.
3. Mary is exhibiting typical teenage rebellion against society.
4. Mary is obviously miserable inside as shown by her unkempt appearance and is probably not "right with the Lord".

Although these answers might be true in some instances, the chances are that, since Mary is an MK, she is just acting according to her own convictions.

COMMON MK VALUE - Beauty is found on the inside, not on the outside. Outward appearance is unimportant and is at least a lower priority than many other things.

EXPLANATION

(a) As a child Mary may have had only secondhand clothes. If she was raised in a village her parents may have found many activities to be far more important than choosing what their little girl should wear. Her clothes may have been far better than any the nationals wore. Frequently washing one's hair has little purpose in the jungle.

(b) Later, at school, none of her friends could afford to get haircuts or makeup. Neither did they see it as important since there was no TV to imprint them daily with glamorous made-up images. In a small close group with little outside pressure, competition for popularity tends to depend more on behavior than on looks.

For Mary, this meant that at school knowing what to say, when and to whom, was what attracted friends—not how one dressed.

(c) Parents on the Center paid little attention to looks and there were no aunts or grandmas to say, "My word, how pretty you are in that outfit today!"

(d) This became an even stronger value in light of her understanding of Scripture:

1. I Peter 3:3,4 "*You should not use outward aids to make yourselves beautiful, such as the way you fix your hair or, the jewelry you put on, or the dresses you wear. Instead your beauty should consist of your true inner self, the ageless beauty of a gentle and quiet spirit, which is of the greatest* value *in God's sight.*"

2. I Samuel 16:7 NKJV "*... man looks at the outward appearance, but the Lord looks at the heart.*"

3. The passage in Isaiah 3:16 24 "*Look how proud the women ... noses in the air ... ornaments they wear on their ankles, ... heads, ... necks ... veils ... hats ... charms ... rings ... robes, gowns, cloaks, and purses ... perfumes.*"
Here the Bible goes into great detail on dress and all with a negative connotation.

4. Matthew 6:25 "*Do not be worried about ... clothes ... life worth more ... the body worth more ...*"

5. Matthew 6:28,30 NKJV "*... Consider the lilies of the field ...*", "*Now if God so clothes the grass of the field ...*"
An idea suggested here is that God provides a natural beauty which is adequate.

Although Mary could be unhappy inside, or rebellious,

or uneducated, and that may well be showing up in this and/ or other ways, it should not be overlooked that since this is a cultural value of many MKs, she would probably be dressed this way regardless of her state of mind. In fact, for Mary, dressing UP may be a sign of rebellion; just as it was among American Christians a few generations ago when wearing lipstick was considered a sin. Many MKs feel there are more important things to do than to spend an hour in front of the mirror every morning. For instance, one could spend the time in devotions or in extra sleep before a long day.

MKs come from many different backgrounds and subcultures. Each mission field takes on a few of the host country's values, and each mission adds its denominational views. Young children are especially apt to pick these up since their minds are still in the developing process. Some MKs experience the mission field for a much longer period of time than others. This makes it virtually impossible for one person to accurately define the motives behind any particular MK's actions. Defining motives behind actions is something we each must do for ourselves. For others, we must always give the person the benefit of the doubt.

Realizing that the person we're observing is coming from a different cultural viewpoint makes it much easier to do just that. For example, making an effort to look for the positive view in Jim's case might have turned up this version of the story:

> Jim is a 20 year old in his second year of college. He has had four different jobs because of "misunderstandings with his boss and being laid off due to not enough work." (This is what he would likely have been

told.) Jim's friend Nancy has been having a real hard time lately. She has trouble with homework and has been misunderstood at church. Several times she has really needed help that only Jim could give, (meaning that only he seemed to understand.)

Knowing that he could trust God for his financial needs, he took time off from work to help Nancy.

Jim is not sure why everyone keeps asking if he and Nancy are serious. He really hasn't thought about their future at all and so does not see her as nearly so close a friend as the friends he has had in the past. Of course, he is concerned about her as a "sister", but his time out to help her has nothing to do with romance.

Viewing an MK's behavior as "different" rather than "wrong" will help him to put it in proper perspective so that instead of seeing himself as a failure, he can see his lifestyle as perhaps inappropriate in the new setting. This presents him with a reason to change, and it also frees him to let God work since he can approach the matter with a clear conscience.

In both of the examples above, normal counsel could have dangerous results since Mary or Jim might be led to feel bad about the way they are without being shown why they can or should be different. In order for them to change, they would first need to be accepted as they are, and then, as the subject came up, they could be shown Biblical or logical reasons why a new way of acting might be better in their new setting.

3

When Cultures Collide

THE STORIES IN chapter two illustrated what happens when one individual's ethics or values conflict with another's. Values present themselves in complicated ways, affecting other social aspects of the person's life. Altogether, over a period of time, the accumulation of such conflicts can create a pattern of social rejection. This is the pattern that knowledge about MK values and ethics can help to break.

Here is an example of how several different conflicting values may coincide. It is written from the MK point of view:

Kathy, an MK, is married and has lived in the U.S. for many years. She always had a lot of friends when she was on the field. Now she has a few acquaintances who call her occasionally on the phone. However, no one ever comes to her house or does anything with her, so she feels very unpopular.

A few times someone has asked her to have lunch with them at a restaurant. However, as both she and her "friends" were on a tight budget, she thought this was a strange thing to suggest for an outing, so she declined, stating that she could not afford to go out.

Gathering all of her courage, Kathy decided to go back to the way she had always made friends in the past. She walked up to acquaintance Jill's door and knocked. When Jill answered she was extremely embarrassed and kept apologizing about not having vacuumed, etc. Finally, after some awkward silence, Kathy left apologetically, and Jill did not call again. She tried this with two other friends and gave up.

Each time Kathy attempted to make friends, she widened the gap between her and the few acquaintances she did have.

From an American point of view, Kathy would not have been considered unpopular. She had people calling her. She had some women asking her to go out to lunch. The whole problem would probably not be viewed as very significant. Probably, however, Kathy's failure to call her friend before visiting would be viewed as inconsiderate.

Some States-siders might also have been offended by her turning them down for lunch. Had they known that her income was the same as theirs, they might not have understood her statement, "I don't have enough money", and believed that she was avoiding them. Most Americans would scrape something together for such an occasion.

For Kathy, however, this situation would be a serious problem. Without an understanding of what has been happening, she might go on thinking that she is disliked and continue to wonder why she is so unpopular.

The ethical and value differences here are listed as follows:

STATES-SIDE	vs.	MK

Casual Friendships vs. Deep Friendships;

State-siders are satisfied with casual friendships.
MKs want deep close friends with whom they can share their innermost feelings and who are important to each other at all times.

Time Value vs. Time with Friends;

Just a phone call would suffice to maintain a friendship in the U.S. An MK would expect to spend an occasional half-day together.

Calling Ahead vs. Dropping By;

In MK culture nothing is as important as the friendship itself; therefore, the condition that your house is in does not matter. Whatever someone might be doing they would gladly drop when a friend drops in.

Eating Out vs. Doing Something Free

Many MKs are uncomfortable doing anything which costs money, unless it is a true need or will attain something which will last. Money is not spent for recreation.

Avoiding Uncomfortable Relationships vs. Confronting

Instead of confronting Kathy, Jill simply never called back. States-siders are used to relationships simply dissolving if they are no longer functional, but many MKs, having lived on a small center where dealing with issues is unavoidable, would feel uncomfortable with no resolution at all to a conflict.

[35]

Sometimes, because they express themselves in different ways, values or ethics can be very difficult to recognize in a situation. Here is an example of a hidden MK ethic:

Janie is staying in a college dorm near her aunt and uncle. She lives on campus and does not often need a car. Neither can she afford one. But on a certain day, when a friend is in town, she is also invited to a church party. She decides to borrow her aunt's car and take the whole day out shopping and visiting. She has borrowed her aunt's car before and does not expect any problems. However, this time when she asks, she finds that her aunt becomes extremely angry.

Janie has asked to borrow money occasionally. She has also used her aunt's and uncle's phone to make long-distance phone calls a few times. Of course, she assumed they would show her the bill at the end of the month, but they never did.

One day Janie's uncle goes to the pastor with the whole problem. "These MKs think Americans owe them a living!" he exclaims. He wonders if MKs are just used to people supporting them.

The ethic Janie is acting on is: "Those who have should share with those who have not."

This ethic is partly supported by the following passages in Scripture:

"Bear ye one another's burdens ..." Galatians 6:2 KJV
"... It is more blessed to give than to receive ..." Acts 20:35 KJV

"Give and it shall be given unto you ..." Luke 6:38 KJV

It is also supported by the environment in which most MKs grew up:

On the small centers the missionaries share what they have with each other. They share whenever there is a true need: meals, cars, boats, books, and everything possible. If one person can't justify buying an item for his particular work but needs it occasionally, the others are always happy to pitch in.

Janie would be hurt for the following reasons:

Her aunt and uncle have a car sitting in the driveway unused. They seemed happy to lend it at first, as she would have expected. Why are they suddenly angry about her asking?

They never hand her the phone bill meaning to her that they must have felt they can handle it, but complain about her calling long distance.

They don't give her the opportunity to return favors, making her feel snubbed. (While State-siders usually want lunch for lunch, money for money, etc., MKs feel content to exchange a gift, an errand or a listening ear for other things which may be entirely unrelated. They do not tend to judge the value of favors by their monetary worth.)

Janie would be most hurt, however, if, as would likely happen, she learned through the pastor that her relatives felt she was having some "adjustment problems". She would not have interpreted her situation this way at all. Rather she would have felt that she was doing very well, and that her aunt and uncle were not acting in a loving or communicative way.

Conflicting ethics and values can affect almost every aspect of a person's life. They can cause everything from mild discomfort to a severely low self esteem. They can cause people to disagree or to really hate each other. Some value differences are insignificant, while others may make it forever impossible for a person to fit into society.

The greatest differences between States-siders and most MKs are due to the following differences in ethics:

SUCCESS - This is the most important difference! Americans define success as money or lifestyle. MKs define it as accomplishment or adjustment. The success ethic is the primary motivator behind all human behavior. It affects all other areas. A States-sider will spend his life striving to make money or to acquire a pleasant lifestyle. To say that a man has neither is to accuse him of total failure. Similarly, an MK will spend his life striving to accomplish great things and to adjust to his various circumstances. To say that he has not, is to accuse him of the worst sort of defeat. For example: in contemplating a job overseas, the States-sider would evaluate the position in terms of the money he would make and the lifestyle it would provide. The MK would evaluate the same job in terms of how quickly he would adjust to the culture, and whether or not he would be accomplishing anything by the work.

COMPETITION - For MKs from the South East Asian part of the world this is the largest differing factor. MKs from South America are quite competitive themselves and do not seem to conflict much in this area. Virtually every aspect of American interaction contains some form of competitiveness. Cultures from the East and many other third world countries are exactly the opposite. In a simple example: most States-siders, upon meeting someone for the first time, will try to show how good they are. In many other cultures people will try to lower natural defenses by demonstrating how ordinary they are. Because this is a point upon which relationships often begin, this conflict can create miscommunication in every facet of a multi-cultured person's life.

The overall situation of the MK adjusting to the U.S. can be illustrated with a chart. The chart on the following page shows what is occurring in the conflicts that MKs face, and how serious a problem such conflicts can become. It shows the progression that occurs in some MKs' lives as they adjust to the United States, and how that negative pattern can be changed. The rest of this chapter is about this chart. Please refer back to it as you read through the chapter.

MK ACTION	TYPICAL RESPONSE	PREFERRED RESPONSE
Level 1 A	B	C
• Doesn't bring money to a party. • Leaves dinner during football game. • Doesn't wear makeup to church. • Doesn't go to pizza party. • Excels in swimming, canoing. • Can't skate. • Borrows when in need.	• Misunderstandings. Comments and incorrect conclusions such as; "free-loader", "snob", "wouldn't understand us", "He's not my type", "He's naive about our fast-paced world", "He's a loner", "A leech" • General feeling of difference.	• Understand that there is a cultural difference and respect rather than judge. • Provide MK activities and opportunities to learn States-side culture. • 1 Corinthians 13:7 says *"Always expect the best ..."* • Use extra communication skills: literal language!
Level 2		
[Feelings; loneliness frustration, rebellion] • Turns down family dinner. • Goes to a different church. • Avoids youth group. • Gets involved with secular or "off the wall" groups. • Takes daring trips.	• Considered socially maladjusted, cliqueish, irresponsible, immature. A matter for prayer. • Church and relatives feel legitimately responsible leading to gossip. • People pull away, rather than try to "help", since their "help" is not usually effective.	• Use extra communication skills. • Educate; Re-entry seminars for MKs and cultural seminars for others to help with value sorting • Expect the best • Confront with an open ear of respect. • Meet with others of same culture for support • See discussions in this book on success.

MK ACTION	TYPICAL RESPONSE	PREFERRED RESPONSE
Level 3 A	B	C
[Feelings; "I'm different", "I don't fit in anywhere", "What can I do with my talents and future?" Depression, loss of self-esteem, Lack of identity.] • Stress reactions to failure, due to MK success ethic; "To do well and adjust."	• Avoidance. • Consider the MK a non-Christian, not normal, strange, emotionally unstable. • Recommend counseling.	• MK should return to home environment. • Realize success as obedience to God's will. (not accomplishment or adjustment.) Realize that God has a place for the MK, perhaps in helping to broaden Americans culturally. • Continue to accept each other even without change • Expect the best.
CULTURALLY INAPPROPRIATE BEHAVIOR	NOT ALLOWING FOR CULTURAL DIFFERENCES	RECOGNIZING AND ACCEPTING CULTURAL DIFFERENCES

Level 1 represents the first two years that an MK is in the U.S. At this point he may experience some culture shock and homesickness, but psychologically and Spiritually, he is usually fine. He is doing as he feels is right and expecting to fit in better and find people who understand him in the future. MKs in this category, when asked, do not usually feel that they are having any problems adjusting.

In the first two years, people need to recognize the difference in culture and make all kinds of allowances. They should always assume that each other means well, as is directed in 1 Corinthians 13:7 NKJV "*Love hopes all things ...*"

[41]

1 Corinthians 13:5 TLB also says; "*Love ... is not irritable ...*", and, 1 Peter 4:8 NKJV "*Love will cover a multitude of sins.*" People should try to show respect for both cultures, even considering both to see whether the other person's might be better in some ways than their own. When a problem does occur between them they must try to talk about it in an open, honest, literal way.

Misunderstandings in Level 1 lead to Level 2.

Level 2 represents the next two or three years of an MK's life. As a result of the way that people have misunderstood him for a couple of years now, he begins to feel frustrated. He is also feeling some rebellion, since those who have been looking down on him have been behaving at the same time in ways that he feels are immature, leaving him with the impression that they are hypocrites.

Because these types of responses all have to do with failed expectations, it is worth noting here that this process is more evident between MKs and other Christians. Non-Christians do not have high expectations and so are not usually disappointed in the MK's behavior. Nor does the MK expect them to live up to any standards so that he does not consider them hypocritical. The same amount of misunderstandings may occur between them, but the response on both sides will be different. This is one reason why many MKs find themselves more comfortable in worldly settings than they do with the church (i.e., public colleges vs. Christian colleges) and why they sometimes get involved with other groups who are considered to be "off the wall" by mainstream society.

The MK who has been misunderstood and vaguely criticized for a few years will begin to need some sort of mode for escape. Usually subconsciously at this stage, he will look for ways to avoid the types of responses he has been getting. He may go to another church. Or he may avoid various meetings and family get-togethers. If he has the chance, he may love to get away on a trip or do something he might have done on the field like motorbike across country. MKs at this stage when asked, often express dissatisfaction with others around them but would not consider themselves to be having any adjustment problems.

In response to this new more "rebellious" behavior by the MK, fellow U.S. Christians will take on an even more negative view. If they are feeling at all responsible to the MK's parents, they will even take some sort of action—such as making it a public prayer request. If the MK feels that the States-sider needs more prayer than he does, this may alienate him even more. When State-siders are unable to help in any way they will often pull away. Young people may stop inviting him to parties, especially if he usually doesn't come anyway. In general, most people will feel that he is quite maladjusted.

During the first 2-3 years after exiting from the field, (level 2), the primary response should be the same as at level 1, with each party accepting the other as they are. In addition, when an MK reaches level 2, conflicts are usually pronounced enough to create motivation for cultural education. As subjects arise, MKs may be shown *Biblically* and *logically*, why some of their actions may not be helpful in the U.S. This is the time when re-entry seminars may be most appropriate and appreciated. Here is when value-change counseling or coaching could be most helpful. States-siders involved could also benefit by cultural education such as is provided by this book.

By this time, the MK has probably been away from others of his culture long enough that he may need some reminders of home and visits with friends. Such visits will help remind him why he is different and that different doesn't necessarily mean wrong, so that he is less likely to see himself as a failure. MKs should also try to find some kind of recreation which might help them to alleviate stress, since often the stress-reducing methods they once used are often not possible in the U.S.

The correct responses in levels 1 and 2 may help to prevent level 3 altogether. However, it is unlikely that all of the people around every MK will make this effort, so if you or someone you know has reached this stage; here are some things to do:

In column A is a list of common MK actions.

Column B represents the way people in churches, Christian schools, and families, usually respond to the behaviors in Column A. In response to the slightly inappropriate behavior which most MKs exhibit in the first year or two, many people adopt the view that the they are immature, naive and different.

In Column C of the chart, I have listed some ways in which people should respond to missionaries' kids in their various stages of adjustment. They also demonstrate how MKs should respond to States-siders and the attitudes which they should show towards

[44]

themselves. Like any conflict between two parties, both sides need to be considerate of the other.

Literal language - When speaking cross-culturally, even when the culture is only a subculture of ours, we must speak literally. We must try to say exactly what we are thinking, using no hints and making no assumptions. There are always many hidden messages which are implied in the language used by any given culture. These messages are often so well hidden that although people within the same subculture usually receive the whole of their intent, they often do not consciously understand the meanings themselves and cannot teach them to others.

For example: Even such simple statements as "How are you?" carry a much different meaning than what they literally say. A person of a slightly different subculture than that of the average American, would be making a mistake in taking this phrase literally. Most of the time the person asking, "How are you?" does not want to know actual details about how the person they have asked is doing. Usually he is expecting you to simply answer, "fine." This question might be more accurate if it was worded thus: "At the moment, is everything basically OK for you? — Or is there something really important which you would like me to know about before we move on or get to the real business at hand?" When this phrase is meant literally, the tone, the context, or a back-up sample question is often used to convey the nature and scope of the desired answer, such as "How is it going with your new job?" Of course, we shouldn't use words with double or hidden meanings.

Literal language, as developed, enables one to begin to understand all kinds of people from all kinds of backgrounds, even within the United States. When you describe to others exactly what you see, or are hearing, and how that makes you feel or think, you give others a chance to explain their motives. When you tell people literally what you want instead of expecting them to "know better" you minimize the opportunities for miscommunication.

Above all else, let the MK know **you believe in him**. This is the most efficient way to break the cycle of level 3. No matter how depressed an MK is, if he feels that he is a failure, remind him that he is not! Remember, chances are the reason he thinks he is a failure in the first place is because others maintain the attitude that he is maladjusted, which to him means failure! God does not define success the same way we do!

Only if the MK knows that you respect him and think he is important and valuable, will he be able to listen to your advice. Even if you feel the situation is serious, or he is suicidal—and counseling is a must—make sure that you suggest it in positive way and that he understands that you feel he is a wonderful, valuable person, but could perhaps benefit even more from the good advice that people have been getting from _____ (name of counselor).

Virtually all the actions in column A (especially in the first two levels) are *culturally* inappropriate behaviors in the United States. If they were carried out overseas they would be seen as honorable and even noble actions. All the reactions in the first half of Column B, however, are reactions which don't allow for cultural differences. All the actions in Column C, are actions which do allow for cultural difference. It may be also interesting to note that the difference between the positive responses and negative responses in every case is the difference between action and reaction. When we take "action" we often do what is right. When we just allow ourselves to "react" to others, we often end up hurting others.

The real problem in this case, is that people—including both States-siders and MKs—are so trained by their culture that they often do not bother to evaluate their actions at all. They simply take for granted that their culture is right, and that if they were doing something wrong it would be noticeable to both themselves and others. They have no idea how limited all cultures can be, and even how unloving their own culture can be. Everyone can see the shortcomings in the cultures of others. To those in the West using bribery in South America, female circumcision in Africa, and polygamy are all appalling. It is hard for States-siders to comprehend that persons from the U.S. are equally away from goodness when they regularly condone such things as materialism which are appalling to others!

Only God knows what is truly right in every situation. That is why it is so important to place Him in the center of our lives! With Christ in control we can relax and trust; not our culture, nor ourselves, but Him.

Level 3 represents the MK who has been here for 5 years or more. For several years now, he has been held as sort of a "case" by some of those around him. As much as he has tried to find his place, he is still being misunderstood, and even worse, accused of not adjusting—which in his value system constitutes the worst sort of failure. This time period often coincides with graduation from college, making things even worse as he attempts to step into a career completely different from all of his childhood dreams.

In the response column (B) we see that as people sense the depressed attitude that he may be feeling they are going to feel more than ever that something is wrong with him. This will tend to increase their subconscious avoidance and cause them to act so different around him from how they normally act, that he will no longer be able to learn from them how to act in American culture. (Please note that these are not usually overt actions, but subconscious responses.)

All of this will make the MK even more sure that he is a failure. It will decrease his chances of fitting in with the church. MKs in this level of Christian society often avoid church altogether in order to avoid being judged.

Many MKs who have been in the U.S. for more than five-years will tell you that they are having problems. They may place the blame on their past, themselves, or others, but most would agree that life has become extremely difficult in the U.S. at some point or another for them.

In the end level 3 becomes a vicious cycle. The response increases the negative feelings, which increases the negative response, which in turn causes more negative actions and feelings, and so on.

I have seen some MKs get involved with groups, such as "druggies", who are completely accepting of them, the main reason being that such persons were devoid of any true concern. They survived emotionally because the people around them were not prone to judge them.

On a positive note, not all MKs are forced into this negative spiral at all! Many others, by the grace of God, have been surrounded by Godly people who were able to show unconditional love and Godly acceptance. Some for the simple reason that they were multi-cultured people themselves at one time or another. Other MKs have fared well because they had already been taught some of the principles in this book which have to do with sorting values and trusting Christ to direct you.

4

Sentenced to Life in the U.S.

HERE ARE SOME of the circumstances commonly experienced by the "Traditional MK":

The Traditional MK will have spent most of his childhood and teen years on a foreign mission field, including a cumulative total of several years in a boarding situation at school.

He or she would have spent two or three years on furloughs, usually one in the primary years and another in junior high. These may have been fairly unsettled times due to his parents having to travel around the country to different churches to raise financial support.

This MK's field (Africa, Southeast Asia, the South Pacific or South America) will be fairly isolated from American culture (as compared with North America or Europe).

This person will have had a reasonably happy childhood

and be well adjusted in his culture by the time he is ready to leave home for college at approximately 17 to 19 years of age. At this time he will fly to the U.S. with family or friends or even alone.

The Traditional MK will take up residence in the U.S. either with relatives or in a college dorm. It may be one to four years before he sees his parents again.

Realistically no one MK's life is likely to be just exactly like that of this "traditional MK", but these are all fairly common experiences. A significant change in any of the factors mentioned in this list and/or individual personality would alter an MK's adjustment experience and reaction.

Three major obstacles face most MK's upon returning from the field where they have been raised, to the "home country" for college. Each of these could present a problem in itself for any normal healthy teenager, but compounded they present an obstacle of massive proportions.

1. The foremost problem the MK faces as he returns to the "homeland" can be summarized as a complete separation—a separation from all that he has ever known, including all relationships, culture, values, environment, personal skills, ability to relate to others, and material goods. This separation also includes food and climate, which require a physical adjustment. The MK will even experience a separation from some of his old ethics which will require spiritual change. This separation can be compared to a "death" experience since from an eighteen year old's point of view it is quite permanent.

The MK's friends are usually scattered to many parts of the world so it is not likely that he will see many of them again.

Some of the MK's values, culture, and beliefs may never be functional again since they are unique to his mission base or school.

As the MK leaves his country, he believes he will never return. He has been told "perhaps in at least five years if it is God's will." Most MK's have a subconscious feeling (perhaps derived from their parent's experience) that God's will is usually to send you away from your home. Therefore, the idea that it would be God's will for him ever to return appears somewhat unlikely and may not be true. Mission work is sometimes the only occupation which could bring him back, so the chance may appear remote. In addition, five years at this age level is a length of time beyond comprehension. It is approximately one third of an 18 year old's remembered past. Since people tend to measure time by the years they have put behind them, five years would be overwhelming.

The average MK will probably never return to his parents for any extended length of time. By the time his parents come back from the field, a few years later, he will have undergone so many personal changes to fit into his new environment that he will no longer be able to relate to his parents in the same way that he did before leaving. Furthermore, living with his parents would be more difficult because by that stage he will have become quite independent, and his parents will probably have to spend much time traveling while he will be settled in a job or in school.

Thus, what may appear on the surface to be merely a separation, can be best understood as a death from the MK's perspective since it is a total and permanent loss of most of what he has known. The response either way is similar since to adjust to either, one must go through the same four stages: shock, denial, anger and/or depression, and finally acceptance. When the MK arrives in the "home" country, he begins to experience a death to his entire past life.

It is one thing to experience this death or separation syndrome in relation to one or several things at a time, but it is another thing entirely to experience it in relation to everything at once. This loss is far more encompassing than most people realize. Not only does the separation include family, country, belongings (most bring back very little) and friends, but abilities, appearance, actions and ways of speaking will also have suddenly become inappropriate, thus affecting the very essence of who he is.

The group of friends from which the MK will have just been separated will probably have been as close as brothers and sisters to him. In many instances he will have lived with them off and on in dormitories and spent at least eight hours of every weekday with that same small group for as long as ten or twelve years. These friends will have been a family to him and will have been a deep and serious part of his life! In fact, many MK's find that by the end of high school their entire life revolves around these friends, who have always been available even when parents must be absent.

If an MK is from a distant field or a field where missionaries are in hiding, the past is thoroughly and suddenly truncated. Contact with the field environment is scant or non-existent, and communication awkward.

No one in the new environment wants to hear or discuss anything about the MK's country of upbringing because they are unable to relate to something so foreign. (If he was a native he might at least be interesting!) So, there is, in fact, very little to remind the MK that his past environment even truly exists! Even the sky is a different color.

Everything is cut off so suddenly and completely, instead of comprehending what is happening so as to be able to gradually look for appropriate ways of coping, the MK often goes into shock.

At one moment, an MK's life was going along much as he had always known it, then suddenly, instantaneously, (in three days of jet lag!) it all disappeared! This lack of contact with past experience is one of the biggest contributing factors to the whole MK adjustment syndrome. In fact, it is losing contact with the world with which the MK has learned to relate (BEFORE he learns to relate to the new world), which sets the stage for total self doubt.

The MK has suddenly lost all association with past experience on which to base the fact that it even existed! He finds that he is quite different from those around him in the new world, but because his past seems vague and unreal, his reasons for being different are unclear even to himself and he begins to wonder whether his shortcomings are his own fault. Now when well-meaning friends and authorities tell him he ought to "be like this" (or "act that way" or "dress ..." etc.), he loses sight of the reasons why he is like he is in the first place. He finds that many of his actions are inappropriate, but he does not realize that this is because they were developed for a different culture. Therefore, he feels a tremendous sense of failure at his inability to fit in with other Americans. No one else realizes that it is because of his culture that he is so different, since they don't have the slightest idea what his past was like. Nothing reminds him that he once fit in.

When logic helps the MK reason that "he grew up a different way with different people and that is why he "can't get it together," there is an underlying fear which says, "*If I spent 18 years learning to function with the world around me once, what is to say that if I do start over it won't all change again!*" This reasoning is a logical source of suicidal feelings experienced by some MKs.

The need to view the old environment in order to adjust to the new can be compared with the need for a person to see a deceased friend at least once after he or she has died. Many doctors now even recommend that parents of stillborn babies be able to see and hold the baby, since a tremendous difference in the ability of the parents to adjust psychologically has been observed. This is why very often even one return trip to the appropriate field causes a tremendous change in an MK's ability to cope from then on! Also, healthy reminders of life before the change, from visits with MKs from similar fields can serve a similar purpose on a much smaller scale.

The sudden massive separation has a devastating effect on many MKs' self esteem, especially in light of the problem which I have just described. Not only is everything about the MK different from his new peers, but it appears to be almost all inferior.

When an MK arrives, he has the clothes on his back and a few valuables in a box or crate. He immediately learns that his clothes are worthless because they are out of style, and his treasures are of little value! (Look at the vast market available in the U.S.) Almost as soon as he arrives, he finds himself stumbling into embarrassing situations by saying the wrong things to the wrong person at the wrong time! Consequently, he soon becomes known as a person who is difficult to get along with. Furthermore, since his mistakes are ones which others would never make, it is often pointed out that he is socially immature (a myth which couldn't be further from the truth, since he has a far broader range of cultures in which he has had to relate than most normal kids).

Other immigrants may get away with many differences for years. Because they are obviously foreign they are excused. ("Yes, the French do tend to be that way," people realize.) The MK, being of the same citizenship and heritage, is expected to fit in and act appropriately within a few months.

Not only is much of what an MK does and says inappropriate, but of particular concern to him is the fact that the things he has always seen as his strong points are likely to be neither recognized nor of any use. For an example: the "class clown" has previously been able to rely on his humor to make friends (on which he may base self worth). Now in the new culture he is not at all funny. (Jokes, any traveler knows, are strictly cultural and vary from place to place.) Consider the girl who has always been an understanding shoulder for her classmates. Not only does she find herself unable to understand these new people around her, but they don't relate to her way of reassuring them when she does. Both actions are cultural. Take the athletic child: what good is navigating rivers, exploring caves and swinging on vines if he can neither bowl nor follow a football game! What about the pretty girl who is way out of style? Or the guy whose main interest is in media skills but doesn't know a single TV or radio star in this country!

Unfortunately, although this continuous barrage of rejection comes from all sides, relatives and youth groups are among the worst offenders since they have the highest expectations.

One characteristic of most MKs makes this type of rejection or failure particularly devastating. MKs have an incredibly high desire to achieve success. Their parents are usually "workaholics" who have endured countless personal sacrifices for the Lord's work. The kids, while enduring early separations from family for school, and continuous months of traveling and baby sitters on furloughs, have often been told "Don't complain, we're sacrificing for the Lord's work."

Pressure to succeed can become even greater when parents, unable to be involved in their kids' school lives, eagerly await reports from school and from dorm parents on the kids' achievements and social adjustments. From an MK's perspective, the primary measure of success is not financial stability, or a comfortable lifestyle, but doing something well or adjusting to a situation well without help. Consequently, failure or rejection in these two areas could undermine his entire basis for self esteem. Thus, for the MK the separation or "death" process entails not only a loss of someone or something, but a far more serious loss of one's self!

2. The second major problem which an MK faces upon his arrival in the U.S., is the timing of his complete separation and its drastic effect on identity and thus also growth and maturity.

People go through a series of stages in the discovery of who they uniquely are, and how and where they belong in the world.

This timing of the separation experience makes the college-aged MK's situation uniquely more devastating than the major life changes that others such as missionaries or younger children may occasionally have to endure.

In the early years of life, a child bases his identity on his parents. Then gradually in the late primary and early teen years his basis for identity begins to include his abilities and also his environment. Finally, in the teen years he learns to identify himself according to his relationships with others. His environment and his abilities are still important. By approximately 18, his identity has ceased to depend on his parents. At last he is ready to step out on his own. It is at this time that he has finally discovered how he personally can fit into society. He is ready to move out of home and into action.

Once the new "adult" has discovered his abilities, assessed his environment and learned where he fits in with others, he is normally ready to move into the world and to begin to develop close relationships. But when the adult MK steps from parents into the world, he finds that his world has suddenly and completely changed. His abilities, his environment, and his role in relationships—everything, in fact on which humans of that age normally base their personal identity. Suppose a person were trained for 15 years to survive in the Arctic and then got assigned to a tropical rain forest for study? Or suppose after 8 years of med school, a young doctor was offered a position as a technical engineer? However, a job is only one aspect of a person's life; in the case of the MK all aspects of life change just as he is about to begin to tackle them on his own.

If the MK were to return at a later age level, his identity would be much more firmly established and would not be so easily threatened by changes in outside circumstances. Neither would a younger MK (accompanied by his parents) find the change in society a threat to his well-being since he would still identify with his parents and their role. I think it would be much better for parents to return with their young MKs at an earlier stage.

The MK faces a total identity crisis at exactly the time of life when identity is most important. The consequences of this can be far-reaching.

Physiologically the MK has reached the age of needing close relationships. Any relationships already begun in the life before the change are usually permanently cut off by the separation. Relatives are of little help since they have never existed in his culture, and he has no idea how to relate to them. Peers have always been his source of security, but culture clashes prevent intimacy with the new set of peers. Thus, at the time when love and friendship is more important than anything else, the MK finds himself alone in a strange world.

One other circumstance which makes the timing of the MK's separation an important factor in his adjustment is the absence of young adult role models during his teen years on the field. Since most young MKs on the field have usually been separated from the older MKs who have gone before him, he has no idea what he might, can, or should become in this new stage of life! The young adults he meets here in the U.S.A. are quite different (and somewhat boring) compared with the teenagers he has been used to, so he is not at all sure he can—or even wants to—become like one of them. This causes confusion and insecurity as well as more inferiority as he finds himself changing in ways he hasn't seen in other young people.

In summary, at the age when self-esteem is based on identity (knowing how and where one might fit into the world), and when intimate relationships are most important for emotional stability, the MK has neither.

3. Finally, a very simple but absolutely crucial problem which MKs face, is that all that happens to them is totally out of their control. A missionary, by contrast, goes to the field of his own accord. If the job becomes too much for him there is always the possibility that he could give up and come home. If a missionary finds himself homesick, frustrated or rejected, he takes comfort in the purpose of his sacrifices. They are an act of his will. This is not true for many MKs. Through the process of all of these difficulties, the MK sees himself as a prisoner with no control in his life just at the very age when he should begin to make his own decisions. He sees himself being taken away from his homeland. He sees his past being destroyed and himself lacking greatly in social aptitudes, but there is nothing he can do about it.

Imagine a popular young graduate in your church—say the pastor's daughter, or someone equally established—and imagine if a committee was formed which decided that it was God's will for that young girl to spend the rest of her life in Russia. Now imagine that they came to her, told her she was to leave the week after she graduated and told her never to come back. While she says good-bye to the man she had hoped to marry, packs a few things and arranges for a place to stay when she gets there, people there are neither moved nor alarmed by the fact that she may never see the United States again in her life.

When she arrives in Russia, she finds that she is discouraged from ever even mentioning the U.S. She is told that the U.S. is a terrible place to live and that she would hate it if she returned. She is told to be grateful for the opportunity to have a happy life. When she writes home, the answers she receives are distant and demonstrate that her parents have no idea what her new life is like. When she does things in ways that she feels are better than the way Russians do things, she is told "You have been here long enough, and you're a Russian now, so you had better start fitting in," implying that their ways—not hers—are correct. Even when she faces a terminal illness, or has an emotional breakdown, she is not allowed even to think of the U.S. as her home. As an adult in this situation, even though only 18, she has been treated like a hostage, and the effect on her self-esteem would be the same.

This circumstance can result in deep bitterness against God and parents who have allowed the devastating situation. Since neither of these seem very appropriate, the MK may subconsciously turn the anger inward towards himself in the form of severe depression. (Depression can cause crippling, long-term damage even when it is not compounded with other problems such as identity loss).

If parents could allow their kids the choice of staying in their own (field) country, it would be worth it psychologically. As mature, capable young adults looking for a future, most would soon make the decision themselves to return to the U.S. Bitterness would be avoided since the move would be an act of will and not a forced circumstance. Perhaps they might move to the U.S. at a time when they are a little more established in their identity, and thus far readier to cope with the changes. Either way, when the move to the U.S. is of their own choice, they will more easily find the courage to overcome whatever obstacles the change may bring.

The Old Testament clearly demonstrates how sympathetic God is with people in exile from the country of their youth and upbringing. Time after time God went out of his way to return people to the country where they felt at home.

One passage in particular could be very encouraging to a lot of MKs. In Jeremiah's time, the Israelites were also being forced to live in a land far away from home. They, too, had no idea when or if they would ever be allowed to return. They seemed to find it hard to settle down in their new surroundings. God's first instructions to them were practical:

"Build houses and settle down. Plant gardens and eat what you grow in them. ⁶Marry and have children. Then let your children get married, so that they also may have children. You must increase in numbers and not decrease. ⁷Work for the good of the cities where I have made you go as prisoners. Pray to me on their behalf, because if they are prosperous you will be prosperous too." Jeremiah 29:5-7

After this comes one of the most beautiful promises in the Bible:

Jeremiah 29:11,13,14 *"I alone know the plans I have for you, plans to bring you prosperity and not disaster, plans to bring about the future you hope for ...*

¹³You will seek me, and you will find me because you will seek me with all your heart. ¹⁴Yes, I say, you will find me, and I will restore you to your land. I will gather you from every country and from every place to which I have scattered you, and I will bring you back to the land from which I had sent you away into exile. I, the Lord, have spoken."

God knows the Israelites were the same kind of people that we are. He has the same sort of empathy for the MK today as he did for the Israelites then.

5

How MK Culture
Is Developed

"HOW COULD MY kids possibly have a culture which is different than ours!" is the question I most frequently hear from missionary parents. Even MKs often wonder how they could have grown up with a set of beliefs which is different than that of their own parents. Many times, siblings from the same family each end up having a different subculture. It brings up an important issue, since there are some things which young parents of MKs can watch out for while raising their kids and therefore lessen some of the differences. Other things, however, are inevitable.

There are basically two types of culture-forming situations which are **different for the MK than for his parents**:

1. His environment—the community and country in which he lives.
2. His training—what he is taught and what he learns from others (sometimes deliberately or overtly; sometimes incidentally or covertly)

These situations vary considerably from one MK to another, and yet most MKs quickly find that they have a culturally-common ground with one another. Although there are as many countries for MKs to grow up in as there are mission fields, there are similarities between most third-world countries. Furthermore, there are a few types of communities common to many mission situations: the boarding school, the remote village, the small center of Christian missionaries, and the mission house in a foreign city. There is basically one type of training, varying only slightly from one denomination or mission to another: strong evangelical Christian doctrine with fairly strict expectations of behavior (compared with home churches), yet broad minded. Missionaries are often required by circumstances to work with members of other denominations; this and a wide variety of other cultural circumstances foster an attitude of tolerance. What the MK learns incidentally comes from such things as seeing his parents' commitment to their work or seeing their concern for the poor. Some things are learned directly from the host culture.

The Host Country

The host country significantly affects MK culture. The term Third Culture Kid has been adopted by many MKs because it recognizes the confluence of the home country culture and the host country culture to make a third culture. Nevertheless, this has sometimes been overrated. Most MKs (certainly not all) are isolated from their host culture to some extent by lifestyle and in some cases by the fact that neither their parents nor the other missionaries ever truly accept the culture as valuable or even valid. The very fact that many MKs can move from one branch or field to another with relative ease, and quickly feel at home with other MKs, shows how much of their culture is not due to their host countries.

MKs who are deeply affected by host cultures are those who grow up in settings where there is strong interaction with local people. In that case the host country is also the MK's immediate community.

Some examples of the types of values which may be influenced by the host culture are: attitudes towards business which requires interaction with the host community, attitudes regarding neighbors, nuances of speech, social protocol, and world view. In a notable and more specific example, some MKs subtly adopt host country prejudices and resent the fact that they are white.

One very important thing that is often adopted from the host country is the feeling and definition of "home". Such things as the sound of the birds in the morning, the yearly repetition of seasons, the familiar feel of the air and soil, and the sights and smells of daily life on the street, all add together to develop for the growing child a sense of home. A child relates all things to the environment where he grows up. Missionaries who have lived on the field for 25 years still dream about "white Christmases" in December, and still compare roads with the ones "back home." So too, might an MK, for the rest of his life, even without ever returning to that field, compare each set of surroundings with those where he grew up.

Some missions or families have attempted to avoid this by trying to teach kids that the U.S. is so much more wonderful than where they are on the field. Such attempts to make fantasies of the U.S. replace the realities of daily surroundings can only create feelings of insecurity. By doing so, the true feelings of the child's heart are criticized as invalid. Positive things can be taught about the U.S., but the morning sun, the sweet taste of seasonal fruit from the garden, and the warm smell of national coffee will far outweigh intellectual teachings when it comes to defining home in the heart of a child.

The Community

The immediate community in which the MK has been raised probably affects him the most. This is where he learns to interact with others. Even if his parents are very different from the other missionaries, the child must still interact with those around him. That is the purpose of culture: it is ultimately a language, an agreement between people who must relate, as to how to live with each other. Whether the MK's community is the boarding school, the center, or a remote village, this is where he will gain most of his understanding of relationships.

Some examples of the types of values which will be gained from the community are:

- Expectations of relationships: How close must one be before he is considered a friend? How permanent are relationships?

[68]

- Nuances of speech and social protocol: What does is mean when you say, "I love you"? How should you act with friends?
- Personal role: How do I usually fit into a group? Do people like my jokes? Am I a motivator? How and where can I relax and recreate?

On some fields the children are very isolated from adults. On others, children do everything with adults. This can make a big difference in the subculture the kids develop.

On small centers where there are few children, teens are sometimes accepted as part of the adult community. This ensures that they will learn many more of their parent's values than teens on centers where there is less adult interaction.

Children from centers where mixing with adults is minimized, often feel less prepared to face the U.S. at age 18 than children who have been actively involved in adult activities on the field. Centers where children's homes or dorms exist are naturally geared towards child independence. Sometimes half of the children at such a center are away from their families during the school year. Social functions on a small mission base or center are often planned separately for children and adults. I believe a certain lack of bonding occurs when small children are taken away from their parents—both in the parents and in the kids. Instead, the children bond with their peers. Children on all centers are able to be with their friends at any time of the day, causing even more isolation from adults. Frequently they are away from parental conversations which kids in other cultures would overhear. When children are somewhat isolated from adult life, their own subculture which is often quite different from their parents', grows stronger.

A growing factor in the effect of the mission community on MK culture is the fact that some mission communities are changing rather rapidly. The introduction of videos and TV, and rapid increase in organization size, (less closeness); are bringing such "secular" problems as drug abuse, teen pregnancy, and low motivation into some mission communities. Although these traits would appear to make MKs more like teenagers in the U.S., in fact the MKs will still have developed their own subculture. Since TV is rarely if ever a major part of their daily life, the MK finds that their values are still different from those of many in the U.S. Sadly, these kids are exposed to the world's solutions to life's problem, but face many of the same MK conflicts.

Experiences

The MK's personal experiences certainly affect his culture. Just how much they will affect him depends on the nature of the experience. Unusual incidents on the mission field can severely affect a child's culture or life view. Such incidents may not be recognized as trauma because of their unique nature. In Western countries there is so much publicity over life-changing events that it has become relatively easy for parents to recognize what types of things will affect children strongly and what won't. However, the missionary family faces situations rarely encountered by the average suburban American family: Does watching a pig get cut up affect a child or is this just a natural part of life? Does helping in a clinic where many lives are saved, but a few lost, traumatize a child or is it a normal part of life? Many events will not appear to affect the child emotionally at all, but others may change his values forever.

Some examples of experiences which may affect an MK's culture (his beliefs and expectations) and the way in which they might affect him are:

The child sent off to boarding school at a time when he is not ready to be separated from parents may believe that one's work or ministry is more important than one's children. He may later live out this belief with his own children, or perceiving it to have been a negative trait, may rebel and place his own children far ahead of his job. This practice has been replaced with structured home-school programs in most missions.

The child who finds tremendous relief and exhilaration on trips into the wilderness, may perceive this to be the only real way for human beings to have recreation. He may feel subconsciously that a society which deprives its members of this right is cruel or at least very boring.

The child who has an accident out in the jungle and is casually given homemade first aid may perceive health care as a low priority compared with the child in the U.S. who under similar circumstances was rushed to a hospital.

The child who has watched other little children die of starvation may never feel satisfied working just to earn a comfortable style of living for himself.

Teachings: An Uninhibited Gospel

An "uninhibited Gospel" is a very powerful force influencing MK values. On the field the Gospel is presented out of context with U.S. culture ("home" for the missionaries). The very teachings which are addressed most strongly by mission personnel are the ones which Americans find it most difficult to live up to. These same concepts may be accepted readily and literally by MKs to a point which will seem extreme to Americans (including their parents). Not only are they accepted in entirety, but the MK may feel that the missionary parents or teachers are not living up to their own teaching. Hence, missionaries and other Christian leaders are often labeled "hypocritical" by young people being raised on the field.

For example:

Many missions overemphasize that the love of money is the root of all evil. This is typical of the type of teaching a missionary might teach his children. A parent's conviction that "most people" (most Americans) do not live up to the intent of this Biblical maxim may cause him to want to make sure his children know better.

The average MK accepts this teaching readily. It makes sense. He does not hear the constant admonition of society through TV, radio and peers to get more and better things. He does not see his parents agonizing weekly over distribution of their pay check or listen to sermons on the issue from obviously wealthy pastors. Chances are he does see rich people who love money exploiting the poor. He does hear news of the

[72]

big scandals that occur in the world which often have to do with the evil deeds of persons who love money.

From the missionary's, or American's point of view, the MK who has been raised thus will have an extreme view. The MK might actually believe that any time a person desires money he will end up breeding evil somewhere down the line. This may become the part of his culture which later subconsciously prevents him from taking a business job in which the only possible gain is money. Should the missionary parent himself then demonstrate a desire for a nice car, or retire to become financially independent for a while, the MK might consider his actions hypocritical.

Another example:

James 1:27 "*What God the Father considers to be pure and genuine religion is this: to take care of orphans and widows in their suffering and to keep oneself from being corrupted by the world.*" Most Americans would consider this verse adequately applied if they gave a regular tithe and once per month they spent a few hours transporting an elderly widow to and from appointments or fixing her car. An MK may feel guilty if he falls short of donating his entire life to underprivileged persons—that is what the verse literally describes and that is what all the mature Christians he grew up watching did! The first century church also lived like this.

Teachings: The Pendulum Effect

Many of the beliefs which MKs hold most strongly are passed on by parents who are caught in a process which has been compared with a pendulum. They have had to correct their own childhood values as adults. If they have felt deceived by their original way of believing, they proceed to overemphasize the opposite. This often occurs out of context of the original teaching, as in the previous example.

For example:

> Parents learned, "Save every penny you have". Then they become missionaries. They find that they must change their values in order to cope with their new lifestyle. They can't save money; they don't have any! They learn to trust God to take care of their future. Now instead of teaching their kids to "save every penny" they are teaching the opposite: "Trust God to take care of your future, use the money you have now for ministry." They still believe in saving money, of course, in the context of the U.S. But the only thing the kids hear is the part they are emphasizing now. Trust God for your future. This sometimes results in their kids believing it is wrong (it shows a lack of faith) to save money—something the parents would never have intentionally implied.

Another example:

> "Dress for success" is what the parents grew up hearing. Then they go to the field and find themselves wearing hand-me-down clothing. In order to cope,

they re-evaluate some of their own values. They may notice that they can be more effective in their ministry wearing simple clothes. They comfort themselves with Biblical teachings that success really comes from serving God. It's OK to wear old clothes if that is what He has provided. As they learn these things they teach them to their kids. They might say, "Don't be concerned about dress; what matters is how you are on the inside, not on the outside." The kids, having never thought of it as a virtue to wear nice clothes (not having TV and dress-for-success type teachings to balance), may end up believing "Clothes don't matter, and anyone who judges me by my clothes is using poor judgment. Their opinion does not count."

Another example:

In response to their own adjustment to the field, parents sometimes present life in the U.S. more negatively than they realize or actually feel. They console themselves for their lot with thoughts of pollution, crime, materialism and "city snobbery". For them this is a process of making the country they miss sound less tantalizing. For their children, who do not inherently love the U.S., having never settled there, this negative side of the U.S. may be all they hear about. Consequently, they may hate the U.S. before ever even arriving at its shores. The parents, in this case, would be appalled to know that they were responsible for their child's attitude, since they themselves would still regard the U.S. as the greatest country on earth, despite all of their complaining.

Teachings: The Classics (and Very Little Else)

Mission schools are often given hand-me-down books. Out of these, mission teachers carefully select classics whenever possible. These at least are more suitable for learning than out-of-date trends. Consequently, one of the influences on the values of many MKs is that of traditional thought.

Back to The Future

Some of the values which MKs pick up come from the fact that their parents are often a little bit behind the times of the "civilized" world. They go to the field and four years later they are still teaching their children things which they believe, but which most Americans may no longer believe, having been influenced by the changing American society and new scientific discoveries. This becomes truer as time goes by. Missionary parents may make a conscious effort to update their clothing on furloughs, but not to update their beliefs, which they assume are godlier than those current in their home culture (and they often are.)

Observed

Many MK values are simply learned by observation. A missionary may be very interested in sports, but he never watches sports on TV because he doesn't have one. His MK son may come to feel that to do so would be a waste of time. His opinion would differ from his dad's, yet he would have learned it from his dad.

Almost anything learned by a child will be partly learned

by observation. If actions conflict with a value being taught, the child will usually emulate the action. Often this is necessary for practical reasons. The value that is being taught may be impossible to follow. The one that is being lived is always possible.

For example:

> Children may be taught to get to places on time. However, dad knows that if he were to arrive at the village council meeting on time, he would have to spend an extra hour in the hot sun doing nothing but swatting mosquitoes, so he waits until he sees others in the village go. This may happen several times—teaching the children that if there is a chance that when you get somewhere you might have to waste time waiting for others, you might be better off being late yourself.

How siblings can have different cultures:

Just as MKs may have a different culture from that of their parents, so also MK siblings may have different cultures from each other. This can make it difficult for them to relate to each other when they are adults even when love and bonding is there.

Here is one true example (names changed):

> Mr. and Mrs. Jones went to Mexico in 1952. Soon after, they had the first of 5 children. Bonnie lived in a remote village with her parents, taking correspondence courses taught by them until she was in sixth

[77]

grade. After this she was sent to a boarding school in the U.S. From that point on she returned home only for vacations.

By the time Sally was born, the branch had grown, and the Joneses were able to operate out of a small center located in Mexico City. Sally attended a well-organized small mission school. She was always one of the most capable in the crowd, as most of the other children for whom the school was developed were younger than she was. She had strong supporting teachers, and occasionally spent time in children's homes while her parents were away. While they lived in Mexico City, their world was filled with the games and activities which the mission children played and did with each other. They had their own tight little world. When she reached 10th grade Sally was also sent to boarding school in the U.S. Her parents stayed for a full year to help Sally and her brother get started, but she lived away from then on.

Tim, like Sally, and all the others after Bonnie, spent very little time in the village. By the time Tim came along the Joneses were doing most of their work at one center or another so Tim never had to leave home until he was in junior high. He studied in the same small mission school that Sally did and played with the same close group of kids. In junior high he, too, was sent to boarding school in the U.S. He was placed in a private all-male academy where he remained until he graduated and went on to a men's academy for the armed forces.

Jill, the next child, happened to be the only child her age in the small center where the Joneses continued to work. She had a private tutor and never left home until 10th grade at which time she, too, left to spend 2 years in the American boarding school.

The last child, Bob, never left home at all. Unlike the other four children, he spent most of his time playing with the Mexican boys his age and he took on much of their culture. In his older years he traveled from village to village in Panama with his parents.

Each of these children was raised in a different subculture. Although all but one had experience with boarding schools, only one lived in the very different close knit temporary children's homes. Two of the children spent most of their childhood with a close circle of friends which was like a large extended family, while the others did not have this opportunity. Bonnie spent the most time in the village, as well as the most time in the U.S. Jill lived a solitary existence with only adults and no peers. Bob, though never away from home, was the most acculturated to the host country. Each of these children now has a different lifestyle and a different set of standards. They had each acquired a different culture.

For the MK, adjustment to U.S. culture cannot simply be a matter of adopting the culture's behavior and values. To what extent should an MK change his behavior, when very many of the MK's "values" are in fact mature Christianity? Could the antagonism he often finds in the church be in fact bona fide "persecution for Christ's sake"? Many MKs find themselves asking some very hard questions about what Jesus did when his actions were not welcomed by the society in which he had to live.

What should the MK do when he is accused of irresponsibility in not setting up a home, but rather giving away most of what he earns? How about taking in the homeless? What about taking on volunteer work instead of paid work? What about taking a group of junior high kids on a camp out? One MK who did was suspected of being a pedophile. MKs with volunteer jobs are often considered irresponsible or maladjusted. To what extent should an MK change and under what circumstances? As Christians we are commanded to be a "peculiar" people, 1 Peter 2:9 KJV. How can we be "peculiar" if we do not sometimes do that which is "uncultural"?

6

Sorting Values

THERE ARE TWO basic directions which one can move towards when faced with the massive collision of values, which missionary kids face upon leaving the field. Naturally, there will always be many variations in between, but many MKs tend to react in one of the following two ways. Some MKs when faced with conflicting values, decide that either the values they were taught or the values they now see, must be wrong. They either decide that the Christians they are observing in the U.S. are "hypocrites", not living like Christians should, or that the ones with whom they grew up were legalistic.

1. MKs may sternly live out those old "absolutes," which constitute their own personal values, even if they conflict with what other Christians around them believe.

These MKs sometimes appear to outsiders to be rebellious, anti-religious, and by some mission standards a failure. Those who follow this direction to the extreme, may drop out of Christian schools and/or get involved in novel activities through which they can express their feelings without having to conform to others' lifestyles. (For examples: Bike trips to South America, show business, bands, survival farms, etc.) Sometimes these MKs become very successful in the world. They are not afraid to pursue personal strong points even when such pursuit puts them at risk of appearing out of place with others. However, in the end they may fall, losing touch with God altogether; lacking the stability and protection of the American church around them.

2. MKs who take the other direction feel immediately obligated to take on each new value which is placed in their paths. Since it goes against the conscience to simply drop one's old values without carefully reviewing them and deciding that they are wrong, they then accumulate a whole host of conflicting rules by which they now must live. The result is often severe inhibition and guilt. The many guidelines they have to follow eventually rule out most types of creativity, fun, and spontaneity, which are needed for a healthy sense of person-hood.

    These MKs are usually accepted by society and rated a success (although they may be too encumbered to accomplish as much as the other type of MK). Unfortunately, although this type of MK looks good on the outside, the burden of rules they are carrying may be

[82]

impossible to bear, and inside they may be continuously frustrated with themselves, and exhausted by their constant effort to conform. Eventually this kind of reaction can lead to severe depression, in some cases even to the point of suicide.

Marrying a fellow MK, or returning to work with missionaries, might eliminate or at least alleviate this process, as the MK may safely revert back to his or her original set of values to some extent.

The first type of MK makes good use of his talents and his background, but he eliminates some necessary old values, and is in danger of falling into sin. The second type fits in well with the Evangelical community but adds values and becomes bound in rules. Often MKs combine the two, adding values in one area and dropping them in another. Or they go one way for a while and then switch. The obvious ideal would be an overall compromise. That would mean, on the one hand getting along with the Christian community, and on the other, being able to "go for" the things that you yourself believe in. It would involve an exchange of just the right values to fit the new situation. A few MKs have managed to attain this balance. This book attempts to show in the last chapter how that can be done.

For the MK who feels he must follow the new standards, it offers the freedom to realize that many of both the new and the old are not Biblically based, but culturally based. With that should come the realization of a new freedom from a multitude of standards, so that he is able in private, and often in public, to pursue his own convictions without being afraid of offending God even as he might "offend" others.

For the MK who would try to strip himself of all "legalism" and humanly created values, this book presents a basis and a model for conformity which is not based on compliance with "law", but on practical methods of getting along with, or showing love to, his fellow man.

These two principles apply to all Evangelicals regardless of their denominational views regarding grace, holiness, and law. None can disagree that the values we hold which can be traced to human standards and not to the Bible, are not necessarily God's laws. On the other hand, all should agree that the purpose of Christian standards is to fulfill the principal commandment to "*... love one another; as I have loved you ...*"! John 13:34 NKJV

A few points are raised as one contemplates the awesome and daily task of picking and choosing the standards he will accept for himself:

Four principles for sorting values

The word of God

> *"All Scripture is inspired by God and is useful for teaching the truth, rebuking error, correcting faults, and giving instruction for right living,"* 2 Timothy 3:16

Although this is one of the greatest principals to apply in the sorting of values, it is probably the most obvious, so I won't expand. The simple fact is: God knows more about us than we do. If he says it will hurt us, it will. If He says not to do it, don't. He made us. I feel the same way about my computer manual as I do about the Bible. If the manual says,

"Do not spill liquids on keyboard," I'm not going to be foolish enough to wash it because I think it looks dusty. The guy that made this thing knows what I don't know. That's all there is to it. We can never out guess God about what's good for us. He's always right. It never makes sense to go against the Bible.

The only obligation we have is to love

> "Be under obligation to no one—the only obligation you have is to love one another. Whoever does this has obeyed the law." Romans 13:8

> "Jesus answered," 'Love the Lord your God with all your heart, with all your soul, and with all your mind.' [38]This is the greatest and most important commandment. [39]The second most important commandment is like it: 'Love your neighbor as you love yourself.' [40]The whole Law of Moses and the teachings of the prophets depend on these two commandments." Matthew 22:37-40

This is the bottom line according to Jesus. This is the principle on which all of the values which God endorses are based. In the daily process of deciding which action to follow, it is always right to follow the action which is the most loving. God is love. The only time when this rule of thumb is not enough, is when we ourselves don't know enough about what IS the most loving. There are many, many times when the most loving thing to do is to take the culture's, or the elder's, or Bible's word for it even when it doesn't make sense yet. For example: To some adults, sex before marriage seems like love at its highest. Yet when problems of insecurity later in marriage are taken into consideration, it becomes clear that what seems best temporarily is not best in the end. In a different kind of example: To burp loudly after a meal might seem to an American visitor in Arabia to be a very unloving thing. While in Arabia, a hostess might be hurt by the absence of what to her would have been a reasonable compliment on a good meal. Whether from scripture, or from practical knowledge, the real goal of all ethics and values should be love.

Offending Your Brother

> "Be careful, however, not to let your freedom of action make those who are weak in the faith fall into sin. [10]Suppose a person whose conscience is weak in this matter sees you, who have this so-called 'knowledge,' eating in the temple of an idol; will not this encourage him to eat food offered to idols? [11]And so this weak person, your brother for whom Christ died, will perish because of your "knowledge"! [12]And in this way you will be sinning against Christ by sinning against other Christians and wounding their weak conscience. [13]So then, if food makes a believer sin, I will never eat meat again, so as not to make a believer fall into sin." 1 Corinthians 8:9-13

> "The right thing to do is to keep from eating meat, drinking wine, or doing anything else that will make other believers fall." Romans 14:21

These verses are about doing things that other people feel are wrong. Notice that this did not say that no fellow Christians were to be "offended" in the sense of hurt feelings or of them believing that the offender had sinned in the sense that we use the word today. If that were true, Jesus was wrong since he "offended" the religious people of his day over and over again. Sometimes the Pharisees really felt Jesus was blatantly sinning in front of them, even from their point of view breaking the ten commandments, and they were deeply disappointed in him. Rather we must not offend in the sense of causing another to stumble. We must not cause another to sin. Jesus said that if we did it would be better for us to have a millstone tied around our necks and be drowned. Luke 17:1,2

If by our actions, done in our own good conscience, another person is led into action which goes against his conscience, then we are wrong in doing it even if it is "technically right." On the other hand, if we feel that something is right, we need not be afraid of doing it even in front of fellow Christians who think it is wrong, provided there is no danger whatsoever that they might be tempted to do it themselves against their own consciences.

"But the Pharisees and teachers of the Law complained bitterly to Jesus' disciples about his eating with such notorious sinners. [31] Jesus answered them, 'It is the sick who need a doctor, not those in good health. [32]My purpose is to invite sinners to turn from their sins, not to spend my time with those who think themselves already good enough.' [33]Their next complaint was that Jesus' disciples were feasting instead of fasting. 'John the Baptist's disciples are constantly going without food, and praying,' they

declared, 'and so do the disciples of the Pharisees. Why are yours wining and dining?'" Luke 5:30-33 TLB

"When in Rome"...

> *"I am a free man, nobody's slave; but I make myself everybody's slave in order to win as many people as possible. ²⁰While working with the Jews, I live like a Jew in order to win them; and even though I myself am not subject to the Law of Moses, I live as though I were when working with those who are, in order to win them. ²¹In the same way, when working with Gentiles, I live like a Gentile, outside the Jewish Law, in order to win Gentiles. This does not mean that I don't obey God's law; I am really under Christ's law. ²²Among the weak in faith I become weak like one of them, in order to win them. So I become all things to all people, that I may save some of them by whatever means are possible."* 1 Corinthians 9:19-22

"Do as the Romans do." It's an idea that came from Paul, not a worldly maxim. It is sort of a general statement which picks up all of the loose ends. It is encompassed by an explanation, which is a manner of writing, that intones "practically speaking". It is not written as a command and is presented both times in the context of trying to win others. In other words, we don't have to obey as law everything set forth by the people we are with, but if our true goal on earth is to win others to Christ, then part of our method should involve conforming to those others' ideas about what's right, (their culture). That is simple and practical. It is for their sakes and has nothing to do with our acceptability before God.

Jesus said, "... *anyone who does not help me gather is really scattering.*" Matthew 12:30. Part of obeying God is being a witness to others. Being a witness to others does require a certain amount of conformity to the values of those we are witnessing to while we are with them, even though we may not see any inherent good in their values at all.

" ... *In the full light of truth we live in God's sight and try to commend ourselves to everyone's good conscience.*" 2 Corinthians 4:2

In summary

The four value sorting principals for cross-cultural situations are as follows:

The word of God - Does it agree with the Bible?

Agape love - Does it demonstrate unconditional love?

Offending Your Brother - Will it tempt someone who might be watching you to go against his conscience?

When in Rome - Will it create a good witness to those around you?

Note: Each of these could be further simplified into the question, "Is it loving?" That is the only true commandment that covers all others!

Keeping each of these principals in mind, one is equipped to make every decision he needs to, and to create his or her own personal set of values. Flexibility—being willing to change on a daily basis will enable such a person to get along with anyone at any time. But is this all too much for a finite human mind to handle? I have found that it is. I cannot manage it myself, and whenever I try, I find myself on the verge of collapse. On a small scale let me give you one example.

It was my mother's birthday. We were invited for dinner. Wanting to do just the right thing (on a limited budget) I wrestled with the following issues:

"I could give her flowers, but being a missionary she would think that a waste of money since they'll be gone in a week."

"But being an American she'll know that flowers mean that I appreciate her and am not just getting by with a gift."

"But a gift would be something she could value, and you can get a lot of nice and even practical luxuries for $17.00."

"But they do so much traveling, she won't want anything she'll have to carry around; and it won't really say what I wanted to say."

"What I really want is to show my appreciation. I'll give her flowers."

"But flowers cost so much, and surely that's materialism to the limit; to spend money on something that will be gone in a few …"

In the end I gave her the flowers. (To finish off the story with a flourish, they fell and broke apart on the way to her house!)

This is just a tiny sample issue. But the problem is, many MKs must make such decisions all day long. Even those who follow all the principals, make all the right decisions, and proceed through each day with the absolute best of results (as if this were at all possible), may find themselves exhausted from thinking, burned out from responsibility and depressed from a visibly high rate of failure. Like it or not, some of their own decisions will have been wrong.

7

Why Changing Values is Difficult and Often Fails

SOME VALUES WON'T be changed because they actually are more Biblical.

When a person identifies a value which ought to change for the new environment, it may be years before actual change occurs. Say an MK has been logically or even Biblically convinced that he should do something in a new way and he has agreed to change, but when it actually comes down to it he doesn't do it. Or perhaps he does do it once or twice but soon he is back to the old pattern. Culture is never made up of isolated beliefs and customs. All beliefs and customs work together to produce a functioning system.

This challenge of changing beliefs is faced by every Christian in the world to a greater or lesser extent. If someone is raised in a simple village they may have to change very little over a long period of time. People in today's fast-changing world with high-tech media and communication must change much faster than earlier generations. New ideas such as stem cell research and in vitro pregnancies force us to demand a verdict. Even the church must change. Societies must adapt to ever more complexities. Our shrinking world with its resulting immigration problem adds to the issue. Missionaries must learn to adapt to the culture on the field and their new converts must find their own version of Christianity that fits their cultural ethics. The Bible has absolutes but how those rules are interpreted depends on how agape love plays out in a society. It can do so a little differently in each context.

This is not to say that people can just randomly choose what to believe as it is taught by popular "situation ethics," but that in our complex world, how we demonstrate agape love and obey God's commands can vary. And it varies from culture to culture, just as Paul talked about in regard to eating meat offered to idols in Romans 14 and 1 Corinthians 8. These contain a long discussion about how one person could eat meat in good conscience while another could not, because of his culture.

We are all growing in knowledge, "... *grow in the grace and knowledge of our lord and Savior Jesus Christ ...*" 2 Peter 3:18 NKJV. We have the Holy Spirit to guide us into a better understanding of how to love every day. We Christians attend Bible studies to make sure what we are learning is in line with the Word of God. People who don't face moral challenges in their Christianity aren't growing!

MKs must change a lot of ethics and values, in a matter of months. The MK's environment is changing fast and furiously. His situation can be extremely complex. Ethic and value changes come tumbling at him one on top of the other in a conflicting jumble of challenges and ideas. What may be viewed as procrastination, irresponsibility, indecisiveness, etc., probably has some very legitimate reasons behind it. Two of these are priorities and lack of skill. Priority is the most common reason.

What if an MK is told that he must wear nicer clothes for his job? Faced with potential job loss he agrees. But now he must buy these clothes. Perhaps he can be convinced that it is worth the expense. When it is time to buy them he has $100, but he has promised to support a ministry in which people are starving for lack of a few dollars. He also is saving for a car. Most Americans would buy one on credit, but he believes he must pay only with cash. He is low on groceries. His friends want to go on a retreat with him and share expenses (friends are of utmost importance to MKs). He decides not to buy the clothes after all, (or not this month—but next month the story is the same.) It is a matter of priority.

Say the MK is absolutely convinced, after a few embarrassing incidents, that he must never be late to meetings. The next week he is due at a church business meeting at 6:30. At 5:45 he is prepared, but on his way out the door a friend whom he hasn't seen in years calls. If he tells his friend to call back later, according to MK culture he believes the friend might take it to mean "I don't want to relate to you," and would consequently be offended. Everyone at the business meeting goes to his church. Surely, they will understand if he is absent for the first few minutes. The first few minutes of a church meeting in America are normally occupied with small talk anyway; something an MK considers a waste of time. Faced with all of this he decides to talk to his friend "just long enough to let the other person know he cares." He is twenty minutes late as usual.

Values usually work together in clusters. It can be very difficult or even impossible to change one little value in a cluster without upsetting the security of the whole cluster. It can cause a lot of stress and may take a lot of time.

For example, perhaps an MK has become convinced that he or she should get involved in church activities in order to make more friends. She sees that she might need to conform a little to their way of life in order for them to relate to her. But, now, what about her clothing? She may not be ready to change that yet. And what about small talk? Is she ready to see that as anything other than putting on a mask? What about the expensive fees charged by the church for activities? Is she ready to pay for recreation in a church, when she has always felt that recreation with fellow believers was a God-given right? Each of these values is suddenly brought into focus because of her decision to conform a little more to the new culture in just one area. Most MKs are willing and able to change in several areas at once, but each time the stress level builds higher, and all humans are limited in the amount of stress they can take. This example illustrates the principle that when a person tackles a cultural change in just one of his values, many other values will immediately be challenged.

Another reason why someone may not be capable of immediate change has to do with necessary skills. If one is unable to change because he is lacking in necessary skills, it can put him in an extremely embarrassing position. This is worth discussing because often the situation may become too embarrassing, for the person who must change, to handle or address without extremely supportive and sensitive friends. Some examples of skills which are embarrassing for adults to learn are;

Driving a car - Some MKs were never in a position to need to drive a car. Suddenly their husband dies, or they must get a job away from college and they do not know how to drive.

Putting on makeup - Many MKs grew up believing that makeup was a waste of time and that it simply covered up a person's own natural God-given beauty. People may even have offered to teach the MK how to use makeup in high school, but because of her circumstances it may have seemed frivolous to the MK teen and she may have turned it down. Now, as an adult, for her job's sake she must learn, but where can she admit that she doesn't even know what "rouge" or "blush" mean, let alone that she needs to be shown how to use them.

Buying food in a restaurant - Where do you pay? When? How do you leave a tip on a credit card?

Another problem which concerns necessary skills is more subtle and therefore is more often a hindrance. Some skills are taken for granted and no one would ever guess that skill was involved. For example, at a certain point I myself realized the need to become stylishly dressed. I got all of the advice I could from accepting friends and followed their suggestions about watching magazines and newspapers. However, I still seemed unable to get the hang of it. Then one day, shopping with my sister-in-law (States-side), I realized why: As she went through the aisles of a store with me, she made comments like "Isn't this cute", "Hmm, that looks so sexy." "How could anyone wear that! Positively indecent!" and "Oh, that's just so darling!" I was absolutely lost! I could understand about being descent or indecent, but I had no idea what was cute, attractive or ugly. They all looked exactly the same. They looked modern but nice. Then I realized that all of my life I had been taught never to judge clothes according to taste. Not consciously, of course, but subconsciously.

When we went to a primitive tribe, the dirt-stained wraparounds, adorned with bead necklaces and enormous earrings made the young girls attractive. When we went to school on the coast, the simple cotton shifts of the Western business men's daughters were attractive. When we went to American churches the Sunday clothes of one church were to be considered just as attractive as the Sunday clothes of the next, even though there may have been a $500 price difference between them. In all of our different environments we learned to accept people and whatever they wore.

The ability to judge clothes is a necessary skill which typically represents the types of skills which often remain too hidden to recognize that they need to be addressed.

[97]

One thing which can make it difficult to change, even when a person has already changed in his mind and heart, is past experience. Sometimes, things happen to us which make us naturally want to avoid situations. However, there may come a time when we can no longer afford to avoid them. We may have been hurt in the past, made fun of, or simply misunderstood. Our natural instinct is to protect ourselves from letting this happen again. Without knowing why, we are unable to face what we desire to do. It may be difficult to overcome the behavior.

Changing one's culture is a dynamic, monumental task. For those for whom it is God's will, they can claim Biblical promise *"I can do all things through Christ"* Philippians 4:13 NKJV. God always promises to enable us to do His will. There is much more about this in the final chapter. Nevertheless, time, patience, and reliance on God may be necessary for even the smallest of changes. People around him in the new culture usually don't recognize that the MK is having to make these changes. Friends and family members are not having to make changes so they may not understand.

Consider the young man who agreed that he ought to buy new clothes for work. Then consider the fact that he has probably failed to live up to his intentions in several other areas of his life all at the same time for cultural reasons. Or take the guy who is putting his family above his work, and consequently loses his job. He feels a failure for not being able to provide for them but would also have felt a failure had he neglected their needs at the boss's wishes. When a person continually fails to do what he believes is right, he is in a Spiritually dangerous position.

The Bible teaches that we are only responsible for what we know. We do all sorts of things wrong, and the consequent damage prevails, but we are not considered guilty by God until we become aware that what we are doing is wrong. Then it becomes "sin" and we become responsible.

Paul said, *"even though I used to blaspheme the name of Christ. In my insolence, I persecuted his people. But God had mercy on me because I did it in ignorance and unbelief."* 1 Timothy 1:13 NLT

"Jesus said, *'If you were blind, you would not be guilty of sin; but now that you claim you can see, your guilt remains.'"* John 9:41 NIV

We can, however, trust that with the Holy Spirit's guidance, the believer will gradually learn to recognize more of the wrong that we do as sin, so we can realize our need to turn from such things. In this way the maturing Christian grows from "glory to glory" and learns to hurt people less and less. *"But we all, … are changed into the same image from glory to glory, even as by the Spirit of the Lord."* 2 Corinthians 3:18

If we don't realize that it is impossible to sin unintentionally, then we may become fooled into thinking we are continuously falling short. However, *"Therefore to him that **knoweth** to do good and doeth it not; to him it is sin,"* James 4:17 KJV. The person who, in the confusing process of changing culture, regularly fails to do what he thinks he ought to do will naturally come to the conclusion, that like it or not, he is sinning continuously, though in fact he may not be.

Most MKs know that when they do sin that all they have to do is confess and they will be forgiven. *"If we confess our sins he is faithful and just to forgive us our sins, and to cleanse us from all unrighteousness."* 1 John 1:9 KJV. But if their definition of sin includes anything that seems wrong, that the church says is wrong, is a mistake, or cannot seem to be overcome—rather than just what they actually know is wrong—then they can easily come to the point where continuous confession all day long does not set them free. There seems to be no way out. And how can one be sure when an action has moved from "seeming" wrong to "being" wrong in the process of changing one's values?

Satan is the accuser of the brethren. His primary goal is to make people think they are not forgiven. Once he does that it is easy to make them fall out of fellowship with God, or for them to stop believing that God is working in their lives. Satan wants us to believe that when it comes to doing good there is no hope for us. If he can get those around us to accuse us along with him, we may begin to feel unaccepted by our church, school or family as well.

When this happens some MKs get more and more introspective and depressed, but others give up on doing right entirely. They find that they are much freer when they are not even thinking about doing what is right, than they are when they are trying to sort it out all the time. Instead of realizing that this is exactly the sort of letting go that is just what God desires, and trusting in Him to guide them from this position, they give up on him entirely, and put Christianity behind them. They can't make money without feeling wrong about it, so they make money and forget about how they feel. While they are out of God's grace anyway, what will it matter if they make love outside of marriage? After all, "God's rules" (in fact their combined cultural rules) are impossible to live by anyway, so what could it hurt to bend them just a little. And while they are bending them anyway ....

Drugs, divorce, depression, loneliness, destruction; these are the common eventual results of giving up entirely. Yet, unlike many others in the same position, the MK may never once doubt that God exists, or that Jesus is real. He simply feels, somewhat justifiably, that God is impossible to follow.

God would agree. When Jesus said, "*25It is easier for a camel to go through the eye of a needle than for a rich man to enter the Kingdom of God.*" He followed it with "*27... But with God everything is possible*" Mark 10:25,27 TLB. Only God can enable a person to do what is right. There is no other way.

Another source of confusion for MKs concerning sin has to do with the environment in which we were raised. On the field there were often considered to be "good people" and the "bad people." The "good people" were the Christian missionaries, and the "bad people" were of a different culture either as people to be ministered to, or as ex-pats. It wasn't like living with them side by side in a public school. They were so different, that it was difficult for us to see that we had anything moral in common, much less a sinful nature ourselves. This is really bad theology.

When MK children grow up with this situation, believing they are inherently good, it can sometimes be a shock to them when they meet their sinful nature face to face. This often happens for the first time just when they are in the process of changing environments. In the midst of all the confusion and stress, they suddenly find themselves really wanting to do something they have always known was wrong. (What a convenient time for the devil to tempt them; just when they aren't real sure what the right values are!) Perhaps they discover one day that they desperately wish they could hurt someone who has been mean to them. Or perhaps, in the midst of a difficult marriage, they truly and innocently fall desperately in love with another man or woman. Suddenly they discover that they "cannot help" but get a divorce.

Having thought that they were "good" all their lives, they are not used to wrestling with the sinful nature. It can be a real shock. When MKs don't admit to each other that they have those kinds of temptations too, individuals begin to feel that maybe they are the only one struggling with this sin! Like the members of the crowd viewing the emperor's new clothes, each person thinks he is the only one who sees the dreadfulness of sin within himself. Many have never been told that in fact, sin is our <u>natural</u> self. It is what all people can't help <u>naturally</u> doing. Unless we have Christ in <u>control</u> of our lives we literally can't help but sin! *"What **human nature** does is quite plain. It shows itself in immoral, filthy, and indecent actions;"* Galatians 5:19 [Bold added.]

What happens is people don't lean on God, because their conscience tells them that (because of their sin) they are unacceptable to God. Christians know that they can ask God to forgive them and he will, but they easily forget that even while they don't, they are still his beloved children and are

[102]

unconditionally loved. They were forgiven past, present and future.

The fact is we are part of God's family. We are his adopted children. We're not going to stop being a part of that family, unless we insist on leaving it by our own active choice and many churches believe even that can't be done. The only possible way to understand our relationship with God is to look at a parent's relationship with his children.

I had two children of my own. Sometimes they did everything bad they could think of, one thing after another. Sometimes they refused to be sorry, and sometimes they kept on doing what was wrong over and over again. I still loved them just as much, and I also kept on trying to teach them to choose to do what was right. When they did choose what was right but found themselves unable to do so, I was more than eager to help them. Most parents are this way.

Unfortunately, many missionary parents and preachers find it difficult to demonstrate this. They are so eager to obey the verse which says that "an elder in the church must first have his family under control" that they cannot bear the thought of their children being severely out of line. They can easily become more concerned about the way their child is behaving, than they are about the well-being of the child. The child himself may become completely lost in the effort to get rid of his bad behavior. If the child is living in a boarding situation, where the parents feel defensive about how well they are keeping things under control, and no natural parental love is present, this can happen even more.

So how does God treat sin then? What does God do with

it? Jesus compares God to an earthly father and says how much greater He is. If my kids disobeyed me, they would face the consequences of whatever I told them not to do. That is, only if the consequences were not too severe. I protected them from anything which might have really hurt them. I was also happy to protect them from those consequences that would not have helped them to learn, or which they were not ready to learn, even if they really deserved them. For example, I would not let them run out in front of a car!

If my children they kept doing the same thing wrong, I would instruct them about it. I would keep telling them until I was sure they understood. When I was very sure they knew it was wrong, then I would warn them of some form of discipline. The discipline would match whatever it was that they were doing wrong. It was only as a last resort that I would use this, and only for their own good. Of course, I would never have hurt them in the process. Not once in this process would I ever stop loving them, or ever give up on them. Nor would I give them more things to learn at one time than I felt they were ready to handle. Throughout this entire process they were with me, watched by me and loved by me.

In Christ, we have grace to cover us both ways, to forgive our sins, and to enable us not to sin.

The problem with sin is that the consequences are terrible indeed. In this life it is the natural destruction to ourselves and our relationships that occurs when we go against the Designer of the Universe. I have found that most people have no idea how damaging a little tiny bit of sin is to those around them. There is loneliness, rejection, fear, hurt, bodily imbalances caused by drugs and alcohol, etc.

Sometimes we get so hung up on being rejected for our sin, (a lie from Satan), that we forget that our real fear should be of the results of the sin itself. God is our way out, not our condemner. There are times when He must discipline us, but His discipline is never as bad as the consequences of the sin He's trying to teach us to avoid! He wants to help us. He loves us, and teaches us, and laughs with us, and shares His work with us, and takes us places, and shares our play, and even gives us the desires of our hearts!

We Christians are all part of God's family. Those who haven't been adopted yet need only to ask, and they will be adopted instantly! It's never too late. Let your Heavenly Father be a father! He loves you! He just wants to show His love to you, forgive you, protect you, teach you, encourage you, provide for you, and more than anything else, enjoy being with you!

> "[28]We know that in all things God works for good with those who love him, those whom he has called according to his purpose.
>
> [29]Those whom God has already chosen he also set apart to become like his Son, so that the Son would be the first among many believers.
>
> [30]And so those whom God set apart, he called; and those he called, he put right with himself, and he shared his glory with them.
>
> [31]In view of all this, what can we say? If God is for us, who can be against us?

[105]

[32]Certainly not God, who did not even keep back his own Son, but offered him for us all! He gave us his Son —will he not also freely give us all things?

[33]Who will accuse God's chosen people? God himself declares them not guilty!

[34]Who, then, will condemn them? Not Christ Jesus, who died, or rather, who was raised to life and is at the right side of God, pleading with Him for us!

[35]Who, then, can separate us from the love of Christ? Can trouble do it, or hardship or persecution or hunger or poverty or danger or death? ...

[37]No, in all these things we have complete victory through him who loved us!

[38]For I am certain that nothing can separate us from his love: neither death nor life, neither angels nor other heavenly rulers or powers, neither the present nor the future,

[39]neither the world above nor the world below—there is nothing in all creation that will ever be able to separate us from the love of God which is ours through Christ Jesus our Lord." Romans 8:28-35, 37-39

8

From the Outside In

IN MY DISCUSSION concerning ethical and value clashes between Americans and those of other cultures, I invariably hear the question asked by Americans; "What could possibly be wrong with our society in other people's eyes that we don't already see?" This puts me in a very awkward position. Practically any direct answer I may give is going to convey unnecessary and perhaps unqualified judgment on the person about whose culture I am speaking. However, as a multicultural person, who has lived in various third-world countries as well as in Europe, and speaks several languages, I think I can present a general picture of the nature of most outsider dissatisfaction with the United States. The following letter is not to be taken scientifically.

This letter was written before Facebook and shows the

predispositions Americans have to present false selves which has helped make Facebook so popular. Also, the treatise on the importance of style was much more true before the year 2,000. This is written from one foreigner to another, as one American anthropologist would write to another concerning his observations about any very different culture than his own. Sometimes we have to get way outside ourselves in order to really see ourselves. Please do not overwhelm yourself by taking this "letter" too seriously!

Third Day of Moon

Friends
P.O. Box XX
Somewhere Else
Earth

My Dearest Friends (Fellow Residents of Somewhere Else),

In that my stay in the United States has extended quite a bit beyond what I had originally intended, I am finally beginning to understand some of the American customs, policies, and practices more closely. Perhaps you might be interested:

The most prominent difference which I have found in the U.S., which is different from the rest of the earth, is their entire socio-economic system, which is based not on skill, age, or experience, but on their elaborate system of costumes. So subtle is this at first glance and so ingrained in them that they see absolutely nothing worldly or odd about their practice, but rather accept it as reality. People are judged by their outfits. I have heard people say, "If I meet a person without ointment under his arms, I know that he is rude and ill-mannered!" This and all other statements will be translated literally, for the purpose of understanding.

The costumes themselves I find fascinating and most unique among others around the world. In the first place ALL of the women always paint their faces. What is so unique about this is that they do not paint intriguing or beautiful designs to add attractiveness, but rather paint human faces over their own! Each woman designs the particular face she likes, with an occasional slight variation, and then repeats it daily, taking up to an hour to do so. They tell me the object is to be "clean and feminine" though you might well agree that it is difficult to imagine a daily coat of oily paint as "clean" from our perspective. So rigid is this practice of face painting, that I am told it is an abomination in some circles for a woman to show her unpainted face to her husband before she is married. Some are so conscientious about this that they will never be seen without the face they have chosen to wear, even in bed with their husband.

The costumes themselves are particularly fascinating. They are in fact a language. The real meaning of this language is changed very slightly twice per year by the Leading Men (or Women) of the society. These are the very elite of society, and they run the entire country by a very subtle and behind-the-scenes method. Each piece on the costumes, which they in fact design, each color, each line and curve, and each artifact added betrays a certain aspect of a person's character or ability. Intelligence, skill, finesse, sociability, authority, ambition, diligence etc, are all characteristics which are conveyed by various aspects of the costumes. The exact meanings vary every year, so that only the leading Men and Women know the true meanings, and all others are forced to learn them as best they can either as told by the Leaders themselves, or from others who have learned, or by careful observation. People spend hours learning the most recent meanings of these aspects passed down from the Leaders, and continually buy new objects (ultimately from them) so that they might communicate what they wish about themselves to others. The qualities which are attributed to persons with the right costume go undisputed.

The fact is, all who are chosen for advancements, elevations of various natures and ultimately for leadership are chosen primarily by their costumes, moreso than by experience or expertise. This has been pointed out in "how to" books on such topics as how to "get to the top", "influence people", "get ahead", "win friends", etc.

Of course, the same costumes which are worn by the leaders and social elite, are also used by the religious leaders—and adhered to religiously. The religion in this country is predominantly "Christian". However, due to the strict adherence to the practice of costuming, and one or two other practices, it has been greatly indigenized to the point that many outsiders tend to question its validity as "Christian" upon first observation.

The other practice which makes American "Christianity" unusual and particularly indigenous is the addition and amalgamation of a "Cargo Cult." (This strange phenomenon was heretofore only known to exist in a few remote islands of the South Pacific.) The religious leaders teach (and believe) that if people will give to them what little material goods (or in this case money) they have, then God will return to them ten times as much at an uncertain future date.

With these "gifts" the religious leaders build large shrines and the size of these (as well as their costumes), declare the level of success of the religious leader, and therefore the validity of his doctrine. Very little is actually gained for the people by many of these religious leaders, except for the hope that their certain time of "blessing" will someday occur, if not in this life, then in the next, and the assurance that they will in fact be allowed into Paradise which is sometimes based on the diligence of their weekly attendance at the shrines.

Unfortunately for the United States, this particular religion, because it has so little to offer, is not particularly meaningful to many of the common people and religious numbers have been dwindling over the last few decades, since the development of these two characteristics.

Replacing religion as the American source of security are three prominent institutions; Doctors, Insurance Companies, and Lawyers. While not openly in conflict at all with religion, these institutions have gradually taken over the "security" which religion usually presents, and are completely accepted on all levels of society. So much so that a person can become quite in the grip of all three and be unable to move up in society even despite the costumes he may wear.

American curers, usually called "doctors" possess a splendid wealth of scientific knowledge for curing the ill. In fact, their methods might be the best in the world. However, some of the potential benefit of this knowledge is lost in the system. Whenever a person thinks he might be sick, he goes to a doctor who charges him about one day's work to see him for 5 minutes, during which time the curer may ask a few brief questions. From this the curer decides on the correct processed chemical for which the patient may pay yet another day's wage. It is difficult for those of us accustomed to other methods to imagine what sort of accuracy could be gained from this dubious amount of attention, and indeed, actual statistics show that the majority of doctor-to-person encounters are unproductive—some in fact doing more harm than good.

As has been the case throughout history and throughout the world, the curers pay system has been developed by the curers themselves. Thus, it has secured their own welfare even if at the expense of others. Whereas many witchdoctors might charge a goat or a chicken and some yams for a seriously ill patient (the equivalent of 3-4 meals), an American Curer may charge tens of thousands of dollars for a seriously ill patient. However, this situation appears to go unnoticed by the American people due to the presence of insurance companies.

Insurance companies are an absolute necessity for survival in American Society. Whereas many primitive tribes gain their security superficially from religion by monthly sacrifices of one or two chickens to one's gods or spirits; an American adult male responsible for his family will sacrifice five or six hundred dollars per month to his much more reliable insurance company. This insurance company will then promise to pay the curer in case of family illness, or to replace his house or vehicle in case of disaster. In fact, they very seldom replace much of anything due to clauses in their agreements which designate specific items which they will not pay; which too often turn out to be the most likely things to occur.

The third item which has replaced the security of religion in most of American society is the Lawsuit. While this is not regularly needed by the average person, very few people will get by without paying a lawyer sooner or later for something. Lawsuits are set up when one person accidentally or purposely hurts someone else or if one needs to buy or sell a house or a car or other large item. Great amounts of wealth are accumulated by some in these transactions at the loss of great amounts of wealth for another. Perhaps a year's wage might be won for accidental damage by someone else. The Lawyer keeps a good deal of this wealth.

You may recall that when I first got here I was appalled at the way many Americans projected themselves as one better than all others. I have since heard this complaint by several other outsiders. Many of them took it personally. I myself resolved to study the issue some more before passing judgment. You will be happy to hear that I am quite sure that most Americans do not really think that they are better than anyone else, and don't even realize that they are giving this impression to others. In fact, among themselves, the projection of well being is considered a healthy part of relating to others. I will let you know when I find out more about why.

Incidentally, in case any of you ever decide to join this society, I might make some rather obvious recommendations:

(1) Quite confidently the four fields which you ought to attempt to get into are medicine, insurance, law, and costume marketing or designing (if you can ever figure it out.)

(2) You will want to spend a significant amount of time yourself studying the costumes and keeping up with their latest meanings in order to get into these fields in addition to any required education. Success in this area will enable you to get ahead in whatever field you choose.

(3) There is one other field which you might get into which could also put you in a comfortable posi-

tion. It is the one most often chosen by Americans because it is open to everyone with or without education. However, it is one of considerable risk if you have a sensitive conscience because you will have to sell yourself which will require telling little white lies, being fake and keeping up with the costumes. That is, you could go into business. If you are successful you might earn enough to keep the "priests" (Curers and Insurance Agents) happy, plus gain material goods for yourself. Many have. However, if you should fail you may end up at the very bottom and spend the rest of your life toiling to keep these others pleased.

I do have one word of warning concerning this field. You will find that in order to succeed you will have to adhere to a belief and practice called "competition". This belief holds that in your mind you and your product are better than all others and are necessary for other people's welfare regardless of their own financial position or values. You will in fact maintain that for them to value anything above your product would be a mistake in values; and you will have to convince them of this. This is because there are already so many other people in the U.S. selling virtual duplicates of any given product, that if you don't convince them that yours is necessary and better, someone else will convince them that theirs is!

Perhaps you find this in conflict with your own moral beliefs? Well, Americans do not. You might find it less conflicting if you are lucky enough to discover

[115]

or invent an item for sale which has hither-to-for never been sold. You might then assuage your conscience by saying that this is a real need and that mankind has in fact been suffering all these years before you came along with this! Good Luck.

I'm afraid I must go now. There is so much to do and so much more to observe. I hope this letter finds you well and that it has been somewhat enlightening. Perhaps someday I'll be back to share with you in person. Until then,

My fondest regards,

Your Friend in the United States, San Ili

9

East, West, People
and Things

MANY MKS ARE more mature Christians than most others their age. This is because of the tremendous amount of religious education they receive and what their parents are, as well as the wide variety of experiences they go through.

Because their ideas are sometimes more broadminded compared to most churches, and their actions appear immature or inappropriate, so their maturity often goes unnoticed by Christians around them. MKs could be a tremendous asset to the Christian church worldwide if their experience and maturity were more readily recognized.

MKs themselves should recognize their maturity and not be offended or put off by prayer groups and Christian leaders that seem naive to them. Such Christian leaders are not "dumb". They are ministering to a different culture. In some cases, the State-siders are simply uninformed compared to the MK. I strongly encourage MKs to mingle with such groups and to patiently add to their knowledge through little opportunities to make comments, as the Lord allows.

MKs often come from a whole different way of thinking than do Americans. Following are various odd topics which concern MKs and others who are living cross-culturally:

East, West, People and Things

Someone has written a book which places all cultures on a scale. On one end, there are the Eastern countries which put relationships above all else. On the other end, is the United States which puts things above all else. Everywhere else fits in between. This marvelous model explains almost all of the conflicts listed in the reference section of this book.

Most of the time when the rest of the world gets offended by Americans and the West, is because of the value the West places on money. Even the drive for competition, is a product of the value of things over people. Excessive competition in a country where the ultimate personal goal is to have relationships would defeat its purpose by alienating others. Other countries get offended when Americans put their work above relationships. They get offended when they have nice homes, drive nice cars, but don't often feed the poor. They get offended when the conversation becomes competitive and the American audibly builds himself up so that he can gain opportunity (opportunity to make money) or tries to "sell himself."

Most of the time, when Americans and the rest of the world get offended by the East, it is because of the value they place on relationships. The bus driver leaves 3 hours after the scheduled time because he had friends in town who weren't packed. The village chief won't buy a new well and a tractor for his village because he needs his gold for a future bride price and to pass on to his sons. The American immigrant has made enough money by now to start his own business, but instead he has sent it all back home to his cousins. Giving relatives special privileges in government is common.

"The East uses money to get friends; the West uses friends to get money!" This was said by a minister's wife from Papua New Guinea while living in the U.S. In America, friends are often valued for support or resources for emotional stability. People are admonished to "make friends with your neighbors, you may need them someday." In many other countries, money is valued for the people it may attain. A man earns money for a bride price. Friendship is often solidified or preceded by gifts. When the gifts stop coming, it is time to question the relationship. People try to gain money so that they can give to others, so that they will have more friends.

Of course, this principle does not follow exact geographic lines and not everyone within the same culture acts the same. This topic is filled with generalizations. Many cultures in South America are closer to the "Eastern" way of thinking, and Australia is closer to the "Western" way of thinking.

Each culture has its own issues and none of them follow the Bible exactly.

The fallacy of relationships above money is that it prevents economic development, including health, and keeps people in a cycle of poverty which is another form of slavery. The poor person has no energy and no stamina to get out. The biblical command which goes against this is found in Luke 14:26 NIV, "*If anyone comes to me and does not hate his father and mother, wife and children, brothers and sisters— yes, even their own life—such a person cannot be my disciple.*"

The fallacy of money above relationships is that it prevents love. Americans are some of the loneliest people in the world. Our suicide rate is one of the highest. Many, many people are entranced with reaching the top, but once they arrive they find no meaning. Many of the social ills in the United States (child abuse, alcoholism, suicide, and divorce) are caused by a lower priority being placed on people than financial stability. The biblical command which goes against this is found in Luke 12:33 "*Sell all your belongings and give the money to the poor. Provide for yourselves purses that don't wear out, and save your riches in heaven ...*"

Socialism values order above relationship and money.

The fallacy of order above relationships and money is that it prevents freedom. Its ultimate expression can be seen in communist countries where control is required. In order to carry out socialism every significant activity of man must be kept in check. It must be judged according to its value for the whole group. The biblical command which goes against this is found in 1 Corinthians 6:12 "*... I am not going to let anything make me its slave,*" and 1 Corinthians 7:23 "*God bought you with a price; so do not become slaves of men.*"

The value that **is** endorsed by God is presented in a previous verse: Luke 12:31 KJV. "*But rather seek ye the kingdom of God, and all these things shall be added unto you.*" In God's value system, we are to seek Him first, not money, order, or relationships. God is our highest value and He comes above all. He will see to it that the relationships needed between us and others around us will be satisfied. He will see to it that our needs will be supplied so that we will not be kept so poor that we can no longer fulfill our calling. With Him we can have our freedom because these other priorities do not get out of balance. God alone can keep things flowing in perfect order.

Mixing Conversations

The following made-up conversations illustrate the place that putting oneself down, which is an Asian (or Australian) MK value, has on "normal" conversation. Even more important-ly, it illustrates how one simple conversation can hinder the chances of ever developing a friendly relationship in the future:

> Linda, Laura, Sue, and Jill are new students with sev-eral classes in common in a Christian School. The four girls are active in sports and get good grades. They go to the same church and are hoping to foster a friendship. They have spotted each other after school and decide to play a game of tennis. Linda and Sue are both Asian MKs, Laura and Jill are both States-siders. What follows are conversations that show how mis-communications happen.
>
> This is the conversation between the two Asian MKs, MK-Sue and MK-Linda.

MK- SUE   *"Hi Linda!"*

MK-LINDA   *"Hi Sue! How did you do on that test?"*

MK-SUE   *"I'm not sure. I hope I passed but it was terribly hard! Especially question number twenty. That was really a surprise wasn't it!"*

MK-LINDA   *"It sure was, but of course you passed! Don't be silly, you always get A's. I'm the one who should worry. But I think it was OK. I'm sure glad it's over though. Do you want to play tennis?"*

MK-SUE   *"I'm not very good at tennis."*

MK-LINDA   *"Neither am I. I bet you're better at it than I am."*

MK-SUE   *"I've played a few games, but who cares? Let's go get a court."*

Here is the same conversation between the two girls who had been raised in the U.S.;

US-JILL   *"Hi Laura!"*

US-LAURA   *"Hi Jill!"*

US-JILL   *"How are you?!"*

US-LAURA   *"Fine! How about yourself?!"*

US-JILL   *"Just Great! I'm sure glad that test we had today is over. How did you do?"*

US-LAURA   *"Not too bad, but I'm glad it's over too! Do you want to play tennis?"*

| US-JILL | *"Sure! I'd love too! I still have to get you back for that time you beat me at Racquetball!"* |
| US-LAURA | *"Yea! But not this time! Let's go!"* |

These two conversations are very normal and healthy, but they take place in two very different cultures. Here are some of the differences and why:

1. In the MK example, MK-Sue asks about the test. In the second example, US-Jill asks, "how are you?" The MK would want a real answer and would likely ask something specific rather than a general question if she did not feel like hearing about the whole day. The States-sider could safely ask general questions just to be polite and would not expect to hear anything more than "Fine".

2. In the MK example MK-Sue responds with a detailed answer to MK-Linda's question. In the U.S. a few more polite but pat phrases are exchanged.

3. In the MK example MK-Sue describes her experience with the test as though she is not confident about it. This leaves room for MK-Linda to describe her experience even if it was a poor one, without embarrassing her. (It could be translated "If you did poorly on the test, I understand.") It says, "I am not competing with you."

4. In the States-side version, US-Jill takes precautions for how well US-Laura did by asking her outright. US-Laura then answers outright. If US-Jill had done well too; no harm done. But if Jill had found the test very difficult she may not feel free to share this with US-Laura, and might tend

to avoid discussing grades in the future with her.

5. In the MK example MK-Linda addresses the details of the conversation (something a States-sider might be less interested in), then compliments MK-Sue on her scholastic ability. This affectively reassures MK-Sue that her caution was not mistaken for a confession of incompetence. It is an important response to MK-Sue's "lack of confidence". (MK-Sue will not say anything more about it as she does not really doubt her abilities.) This compliment also allows that being a whiz would also be acceptable. It says, "If you did better than me on the test that would not threaten me." In this manner all of the competition has been carefully and specifically removed from between them.

After this both go on to a different subject when MK-Linda, or US-Laura asks about tennis. However, we see some of the same differences occurring again on that subject;

In the MK version MK-Sue puts down her tennis abilities. Again, this shows she has no intention of competing with MK-Linda. In the U.S. version, however, the opposite is true. In fact US-Jill deliberately challenges US-Laura.

In the MK version MK-Linda also puts down her abilities; showing that she does not want to compete in their friendship (regardless of the game.) Again, she compliments her. In the U.S. version US-Laura openly returns the challenge, and they are ready to play. In the MK version MK-Sue accepts the compliment, (again demonstrating that she is not really concerned about her abilities) then brushes it all aside and they are ready to play.

Three more interesting insights into cross-cultural conflict can be gained with the examples above:

First, a small picture can be gained regarding the very different nature of friendships between the cultures. The MK version is designed to accommodate real deep sharing, and acceptance of any type of person. The States-side version cautiously tests the other person for characteristics and looks for things in common, with no immediate promise of depth.

Second, insight into the different cultural attitudes can be gained. The MK conversation is humble, accepting, and open. The States-side one is upbeat, competitive, and independent.

Third, by mixing the two conversations we can see a clear example of how MKs often get misunderstood by States-siders, and sometimes vice versa. Even though, as has been said before, the conversation above does not necessarily represent all MKs, it is a clear example of how a few casual words can set off an entirely wrong impression. Here is the conversation one more time with MK-Linda, and US-Jill, the States-sider together so that we can see what happens cross-culturally:

MK-LINDA   *"Hi Jill!"*

US-JILL   *"Hi Linda! How did you do on that test?"*

MK-LINDA   *"I'm not sure. I hope I passed but it was terrible. How did you do?"*

US-Jill is startled by MK-Linda's response, and thinks that MK-Linda is not very smart and down on herself.

US-JILL   *"I did not think it was too bad."*

MK Linda is frustrated at the assumption that she didn't do well and wonders why US-Jill thinks so little of her, she begins to feel a little defensive. She may also feel that Jill is acting like a "snob." She tries to change the subject.

US-JILL   *"How was your day?"*

She is still uneasy, because MK-Linda has not exchanged the normal greetings. If it wasn't the test what was it?

MK-LINDA   *"Well, it started out fine, until I remembered we had that test, and then I spent most of my lunch hour cramming, and after that I barely got time to do the test and it was time to go to work. Now that I'm off I've got a little time though; would you like to play tennis."*

MK-Linda thinks US-Jill is trying to be a caring person even though she doesn't understand her, because she asked about her whole day! US-Jill thinks MK-Linda must be really under stress or lonely to have told her so many sad details. She had the same kind of day, but "she can handle it" and doesn't need "to lean on someone else." What's the big deal?

US-JILL   *"Sure! I'd love to! I still have to get you back for that time you beat me in Racquetball!"*

She is relieved that the conversation is onto a new subject and plunges in, not stopping to comment on MK-Linda's day or to counter it with anything from her own. This leaves MK-Linda with the realistic impression that US-Jill did not really want to hear all about it after all, and the false impression that US-Jill doesn't care about anyone but herself.

MK-LINDA   *"I don't care about that game of racquetball, and I know that you are way better at tennis than I am. I'm sure you'll win, but let's just go ahead and play!"*

MK-Linda is dutifully putting herself down, especially since US-Jill has seemed unable to handle losing in the past, or why else did she mention it? She is trying to remove the competition from their relationship.

US-JILL   *"Well we don't have to play if you don't want to. It was your idea."*

US-Jill thinks MK-Linda has too poor a self-image to enjoy a good game. It sounds like she doesn't really want to play after all.

MK-LINDA   *"I want to. Why? Don't you want to? If you don't want to, we could do something else?"*

[127]

This is a typical ending for a conversation which is fraught with cultural misunderstanding. Whatever way the two girls spend that particular afternoon, MK-Linda will continue to feel misunderstood by US-Jill and to view her as somewhat of an over-confident snob. US-Jill will continue to view MK-Linda as insecure and pessimistic, and having a low self esteem. Chances are both will tend to avoid each other more each time this happens, unless they both recognize that they have cultural differences, and determine to believe the best of the other regardless of how things seem.

The different examples of this brief encounter should explain why even a minimal encounter (such as one church social) may convince an MK that he has no potential friends among a given group and may convince a few people that he is too "maladjusted" to be a comfortable friend.

Marrying Internationally

In recent years, more and more MKs are marrying into their host culture. This brings the whole picture of the MK as a multi-cultural adult into view and forces us to ask the ultimate questions about how missionaries are raising their kids. Much controversy is being generated!

The fact is, MKs who have been raised on the foreign field have only two alternatives for marriage; 1) to marry someone from their very own high school, or 2) to marry cross-culturally.

The first alternative is not as easy as it might appear. MKs who grow up together usually develop very strong "sibling" relationships. It is a very difficult psychological step to marry each other in this case, even if the two might love each other in the very deepest sense. (Think of two adopted siblings in one family marrying.) The MKs who have done this have faced this hurdle in a couple of ways—by waiting in absence for a few years until the relationship has a chance to change, and by a long drawn out engagement. One situation that may work, is when two are given the chance to fall in love from different age groups. However, this does not occur very often, as most kids leave the field as soon as they are near marrying age. When MK schools are small the chances are even smaller of marrying another MK of the same background.

The second alternative is the most likely. Even when one MK spent a few years on the field of another, they are still culturally different, and their marriage will be cross-cultural to a certain extent. Think of exchange students. The fact is by the time people are old enough to start thinking about marriage, they are old enough to have had their basic culture mostly developed. Among cross-cultural marriages of MKs, there are basically three categories.

First, the MK can marry another MK. This is probably the easiest. While their cultures are not exactly the same, they are close enough that with the type of cross-cultural training that most MKs have, there will not be too many problems. However, there is one: In which society will they fit? Neither of them will be able to teach the other how to get along in any culture but mission culture. Yet, not being from the same field they will lack any secure culture of their own.

Second, an MK can marry someone from the U.S. culture. This is the most encouraged by parents and relatives.

However, although it does give the couple the opportunity of fitting in, with the U.S., it also causes an almost permanent unbalance in the relationship. The American (for instance) will always be the one who knows best; at parties, at meetings, in business arrangements etc. That seems to work fairly well when the American is the husband, as women find it less threatening to have to be continually led. But it can be extremely difficult when the American is a woman. It must be added that either way, they will have their own cross-cultural differences occurring between them to contend with in addition to the problem of one leading the other.

Third, the MK can marry someone from the culture of the country where the MK grew up. This is viewed at the present time with something almost like horror. Like all other MKs, except those from the same high school, their marriage will be cross-cultural. It is true that their cultural differences are likely to be greater than say those between an MK and an American. However, this might not make their situation worse. Often it is the subtle differences in culture which destroy a marriage. When cultures are obviously different, intense efforts are usually continually made to search for compromises, and to recognize each other's ideas as valid rather than arguing about who is right and who is wrong

The one objection which is most often presented is that of their consequent lifestyle. If the person whom the MK is marrying has never been out of his native culture, then they may find it necessary to remain there indefinitely. This is horrifying to most Americans (missionaries included) who view this as some sort of imprisonment in inferiority. The assumption is that the foreign culture is in fact inferior. For Americans, of course it would be, for the simple fact that for them it could never become home. (No more snowmen, orange sherbet, pizza parties, Thanksgiving dinners etc.) But for the MK marrying into the host culture the situation may be exactly the opposite. For him having to move to America permanently might make him a prisoner away from home. (No more warm tropical rains, virgin forests, plantains, cajeta, dug-out canoes etc.)

If an MK has spent his whole life on one field, and loved it, and if he or she can find a viable occupation there which is satisfying for them, then this may be the very best place for them to spend the rest of their life indeed—not at all inferior!

This brings us down to the very last issue. Is it right for someone to choose to live at a perhaps less educated and lower economic level than what they have been previously used to, or are presently offered? What about their children? Perhaps we need to look squarely at our western assumption that education and prosperity are somehow synonymous with satisfaction and comfort. Many MKs, having lived with and without both, have come to the personal conclusion that education and prosperity do not necessarily imply satisfaction and comfort. They have decided that they have always been happier walking barefoot over a mountain track for supplies and hunting for food, than sitting curled up by a TV and driving to the supermarket. They have been far more satisfied feeding the starving, and presenting improvements to fellow villagers, than trying to convince over-materialized Westerners that they need just one more product.

[131]

On the whole, the only thing I think that can be safely said about who an MK should marry is that he should study the implications of his choice on his future very carefully. He should consider the cross-cultural factors he will face. Whenever anyone marries, he marries more than just a person. He also marries the person's family, lifestyle, and culture. Within the same community, one can afford to overlook the last two of these to a certain extent because they are assumed to be the same.

There are a couple of examples of this principal which are worth noting. Some MK women have fallen in love with men from Latin cultures and found that after the marriage the men turned to what Westerners consider physical abuse. The men, however, were using the normal method within their culture of maintaining the leadership of the household. In another example, some MK men have married American women and found that they were expected to maintain a profit in business, attain a certain steady income level, and\ or generally settle down to a predictable and domesticated life. These, they had not been prepared to do.

In all cases, MKs will be marrying cross-culturally unless they marry other MKs, and should take responsibility to take the whole picture of the lifestyle and person they are marrying into account; and once the decision is made and sealed, the community should wholeheartedly approve and support them.

Making A Good Impression

For many years every effort my husband and I, both MKs, made to convey an exciting project to the States-side public backfired. One day after the Lord graciously provided us with a States-side businessman for our latest endeavor we sat down and had a long talk. When it became clear to us that his basic goals for impressing others were very different than our own, we each wrote down our top three principles of success. The results were astounding!

Here are the two lists:

Show the Public that:

States-side Ideals

1. You know the project.
2. You believe it will work.
3. Have ability to do it.

Show these even if they are not necessarily true!

MK Ideals

Show the public:

1. Genuine Humility. (Meaning, "Anyone can do it in God's grace, and you're only doing it because God called you.")
2. Sincere Commitment. (Meaning, you won't let anything come between you and your goal.)
3. Spiritual Maturity. (Usually meaning, emotional stability and Spiritual maturity.)

On the mission field, these three would qualify you for almost any task! But these two goals are completely in conflict. No wonder we were so misunderstood!

Point A. If an MK shows humility by maintaining that anyone else could do the job as well, but he is only obeying God, he affectively convinces the States-sider that against point #3, he doesn't have the special ability to do the job. He also convinces him that he may not (point #1) really know the project.

Point B. If the MK shows sincere commitment and indicates that nothing will make him give up, the State-sider may wonder if he really believes it will work (point #2). If it wouldn't, might he be prone to do it anyway?

Point C. Much of the effort the MK spends trying to demonstrate his spiritual maturity, may be a waste of time for the States-sider and may only convince him of the MK's inadequacy in that and the other areas. Although to the MK that would mean demonstrating humility and commitment, to the State-sider it would be unimportant for the job. The States-sider would prefer a demonstration of confidence that you can do it, you know all about it, and you believe it will work.

This is one reason behind many failures of MK endeavors despite their strong potential.

10

Other Circumstances
MKs May Face

MOST OF THIS book is about cultural conflicts and the consequences of those conflicts. Such conflicts are a part of the life of almost all MKs who were raised overseas. Chapter 4 discussed separation, loss, and identity confusion. There are a few more circumstances which might need to be considered when endeavoring to understand MKs, most of which have to do with background. Some of these things probably only apply to a small percentage of MKs. Nevertheless, for those for whom one or more of these things apply, adult life can be even more complicated. These topics are not related to culture, but I feel that I must include a discussion of them, because while working with MKs they turn up frequently.

Missionary Kid Illness Syndrome

A serious problem for some MKs is a cycle of severe illness caused by unhealthy conditions on the field and multiplied by the physiological shock of returning to a new and completely different environment.

Although this pattern has not yet been officially connected with MKs by any one doctor, (parts of it have been recognized by various doctors), I would like to describe it as a whole, because I believe the complex way in which the causes relate to each other is what makes this an "MK illness syndrome". Because I am not a doctor myself, this material must not be used for any kind of diagnoses. Nevertheless, a significant number of MKs who I have met or heard of are presently experiencing parts or the entire devastating scenario I am about to describe. The causes are certainly documentable, and I believe real research is sorely needed in this area.

Causes

Stage one: The Field

Tropical illness on the field:

Dysentery, amoeba, worms, giardia, and other parasites can cause damage (sometimes permanent) to digestive systems and other organs. Malaria, Hepatitis, Flukes, etc., can cause damage to the liver or kidneys. Serious viruses with long-term affects can easily be picked up. These are often rare to U.S. doctors and frequently misunderstood. Some are incurable. Most third world countries have them.

Unguarded toxins on field:

Many countries do not have as careful regulations on insecticides as the United States. Missionaries, especially when they first arrive, used to and sometimes still do use insecticides excessively and carelessly due to culture shock concerning insects in the jungle. They sometimes become overwhelmed by the whole process of jungle living when they first move, just when their children are young and vulnerable, and develop a fatalistic attitude towards certain conditions. "Let's deal with the problem of bugs we have on hand, God will have to take care of the poisons later." For example: One MK recalls her dormitory being sprayed with a DDT laced formula every night before they went to bed! The effects of such habits may not be visible until years later. DDT effects can even be passed on to the MKs children affecting the central nervous system and causing all kinds of health issues for them.

Unregulated serious medicines such as anti-malarials, strong antibiotics and remedies for parasites, are often approved of for limited doses but used by MKs long term. Taken as young missionary children take them, for months or years at a time, they can build up to toxic levels. They can also contribute to an accumulation of toxins in the liver, kidneys, and other organs.

Accumulations of minerals from poor cooking equipment, rain collecting systems, and untested wells can build imbalances of which the effects may not be felt until years later.

Particularly notable in this area is the effect on some MKs of poor quality mercury amalgam fillings in their teeth. Mercury itself is harmless but coupled with a non-oxygen producing microbe such as Candida, a common illness in the United States which often settles in the mouth, it can do terrible things to the central nervous system.

Stage Two: The move to the U.S.

Complications caused by changing environments:

A complete change of diet, habits and activities can be very hard on health in addition to the stress of culture shock.

Changes in an MK's health which happen during the move often go unrecognized until they become severe. New people around them do not recognize such things as a drop in energy level or weight, change in skin tone, etc., since they have not been with the MK in the past. The MK himself may have other reasons for depression and not notice all the changes in his health. There is no familiar doctor to refer to.

An Immunologist who worked with MKs has suggested that the complete change in environment can also cause a significant drop in the efficiency of the immune system itself. The immune system which has been focused on one set of environmental factors such as parasites must suddenly change to focus on an entirely different set of factors, including such things as food additives and smog. The same thing happens in reverse with missionaries going overseas. Whether this is true or not remains to be proven, but what is true is that most MKs with severe long-term illnesses, do not get sick until they leave the field just as most missionaries don't get sick until they get there.

No MK that has traveled is a "text-book case".

Stage Three: The Unbalanced System

This stage can develop as late as 10 years after leaving the field.

Physical weakness from above causes plus stress and an uninitiated immune system leaves MKs wide open to serious illness in the U.S.:

Such opportunistic diseases as "Chronic Fatigue Syndrome", Mononucleosis (which transforms into Epstein-Barr in adults) and Candidiasis or "Candida" are very common among MKs as well as "Fibromyalgia" which causes severe pain. Candida is particularly devastating, hitting mostly young women. It occurs when an ordinary yeast infection gets out of hand and becomes systemic, causing damage to many other organs as well as severe allergies. This can be caused by damage to the intestinal system due to past dysentery or an imbalance in intestinal microbes. Two biggest symptoms are depression and disorientation. Allergies can also cause severe mood changes. Alternative medication may be a helpful resource for such situations.

Mercury fillings can be especially devastating to the body when they break down. While some dentists still shy away from seeing this as a problem (because ordinary mercury is harmless), other dentists refuse to use mercury amalgam anymore. This is how the mercury cycle works: Intestinal microbes become imbalanced (common due to overseas intestinal diseases), Candida, which is a non-oxygen producing microbe takes over and lives in the digestive system including the mouth. There it turns ordinary mercury into methyl mercury which is a highly volatile toxin affecting the central nervous system. Once methyl mercury works its way into the intestines it further kills off healthy microbes making way for more Candida and so the cycle goes on. Symptoms such as memory loss, depression, fibromyalgia and allergies, as well as some of the cases that get diagnosed as Chronic Fatigue Syndrome could really be mercury poisoning.

Emotional Illnesses

There are several emotional illnesses found among MKs. There are of course hereditary mental illnesses such as schizophrenia and Bipolar Disorder (also called Manic-Depression). Naturally MKs are not spared their share of such conditions as Hyperkinesis, Autism and Retardation. However, certain emotional illnesses seem to be showing up at more than the usual population rates as described below:

Major Depression – Depression can be a part of the natural grieving process caused by separation and loss; two things which most MKs have plenty of. When a person loses people, places or things they usually go through a grieving process which involves denial, anger, depression, and finally acceptance. Not only do most MKs have an inordinate amount of losses to grieve, which often spills well into their adult life, but many get stuck in the denial or depression phases, because religion often forbids the anger phase, a necessary step in completing the cycle. (Normally one tends to jump back and forth between phases until the process is complete.) A discussion of this cycle is found elsewhere in this book.

Anorexia and Bulimia – This appears to be common among MKs also. Perhaps because its source is an effort to control oneself and control and perfection are so emphasized by religion. Anorexia, in which one starves oneself to death, and Bulimia in which one throws up after eating or uses laxatives

[140]

in order to starve, have been associated with pressure to conform which is common among MKs. These disorders must be treated by professional experts. Many Christians are afraid of getting help from Psychologists who often treat these disorders, but it is important to consider that these are not Spiritual disorders which would require a Christian counselor. They are disorders of the psyche or emotions, which are part of the body and so it is both safe and appropriate to treat them with secular doctors.

Dissociative Identity Disorder – Believe it or not this seems to be a common disorder among MKs despite its previous dramatic sounding name, "Multiple Personalities." I believe culture change is a big reason why. Consider how a child develops his personality:

First, she learns some new thing about her environment. Let's say she sees a cat. Later she learns that the cat is soft. She adds that to her previous knowledge. After that she may learn that a cat can scratch. This is attached to the information she already has on cats, and so on. Gradually she builds a "file" in her brain, perhaps adding lions, dogs, teddy bears, etc. However, if something doesn't fit the file, such as a car, she may start a new file. Gradually, and with her parents help, she should eventually connect the various files into one big one called her personality. This putting together usually happens around ages 7–10 according to Dr. Wilder, an MK psychologist.

Things go wrong when either of two things happens.

1. If her "files" are not connectable, such as when Daddy who is nice in the daytime also molests her at night. Or,

more significant to MKs, when two cultures cannot be reconciled. For example, "bugs are bad," and "bugs are things you eat." Or "Mommy and Daddy will always be there" and "Mommy and Daddy have gone into the jungle." Another example is "scary men in feathers and paint are bad guys" and "scary men in feathers and paint are good guys". This is a sort of trauma for the child as he can't put his "files" together, especially if he is in a non-nurturing environment such as a boarding school between the ages of 7 and 10.

2. Not all children can get D.I.D. It is estimated that only 1 in 4 children have the intelligence, creativity and dissociative ability to use this as a coping mechanism. With this mechanism, one can live with D.I.D. for a lifetime without severe problems. However, it can also break down and cause very severe problems. Characteristics such as short-term memory loss, loss of time, a need to "psyche" oneself up for even familiar activities, and sudden changes in personality such as beliefs, habits, feelings, or thinking style are all symptoms. Symptoms can also be much worse, including dramatic bi-polar-like activity swings, denial of severe inappropriate actions and total memory loss. When any of these symptoms occur, it is advisable to seek out a professional, either a Christian Counselor or a Psychologist who is familiar with DID. The cure is long and arduous therapy and the patient can become worse before they get better. Some may never be fully cured and may have to learn to cope with it. However, it is worth it if it will restore oneness to a person's soul. A highly rec-

ommended book is "Unlocking the Mysteries of Multiple Personality" by Dr. Friesen. Dr. Wilder of Shepherds House in California and his seminars are an excellent resource.

Borderline Personality Disorder – This is much less common but is worth mentioning because it, too, can be caused by MK circumstances. In some cases there is neglect in the first few years, if parents must leave their baby in nursery after nursery as they travel to various churches to raise support, maintain jobs, and get their Bible education. This is a problem in developing healthy separation from parents. The symptoms of BPD in adults are constantly clinging to one or more persons and being overly dependent on them. Spouses or boyfriends are common choices. The best remedy is patience and nurturing love over a very long period of time—so long in fact, that it was once thought to be a disorder of the personality, as is still implied by its name, rather than a developmental issue.

Demonic Oppression

Demonic oppression is usually considered whenever a person has come out of a background of drugs, rock music, or exposure to the occult. It is not usually associated with MKs; however, I believe it is far more frequently a factor than most people realize. There are two reasons for demonic attacks on MKs. One is past environment, the other is future potential.

In many Mission fields some local people worship spirits. The missionary family is not only surrounded by demonic activity but their work is an attack against it. Some missionaries are aware of the satanic resistance they are up against and are active in spiritual warfare. They pray for protection for their children as well. However, how many teach their children how to fight against evil spirits, or even how to recognize them? Many MK children, having no idea what they are dabbling with, have encountered spirits, or participated in spiritual ceremonies or gotten help from shamans. Most do so thinking it mysterious or funny. They may not quite believe any of it is true, but they don't make a stand against it either. Some missionary parents don't recognize that evil spirits can be real and can attach themselves to people.

I, myself, had a terrible experience where a ball rolled into a spirit worship house. Everyone in the village said I would die if I went in to get it. I thought that as a Christian it was safe to do so. That night I came down with a serious attack of Dengue fever and almost died but the Lord brought me out of it. I don't think this was a coincidence. All spirits must leave in the name of Jesus, but sometimes we don't recognize that we should execute that authority.

Many missionaries do not even believe in evil spirits. The Bible makes it very clear. *"For we wrestle not against flesh and blood, but against principalities, against powers, against the rulers of the darkness of this world, against spiritual wickedness in high places."* Ephesians 6:12 KJV

There are numerous references to evil spirits in the Bible and Jesus cast out spirits about as often as he healed the sick. Nevertheless, some who go to the field are not really aware of the reality of the battle which they are fighting. They still fight in the name of the Lord, so I suppose it does not matter—they themselves are trusting in Jesus. But what about their children? What if their children are not even saved? They walk among the villagers, even more than the parents. Many times, kids are invited to ceremonies where parents are not welcome. Many MKs have seen supernatural things take place that they would never dare to report. This can be a source of nightmares. If a child is actually demonized, it can lead to a strong temptation to sin in adulthood. Demons cannot possess the believer, but they can harass and tempt. Sex addiction is a besetting sin that can often be traced to demonization.

Satan also knows the potential of the MK. He may not be able to predict the future, but he isn't stupid. The skills and the knowledge of God's word that most MKs have is a tremendous threat to him and his kingdom. Satan knows that when MKs are free to minister, they do not have many cultural barriers holding them back. He knows that if they were to go to the field, their minds and bodies would not require years to adjust before they could be affective. He knows that with their level of self-motivation, they could go far in almost any direction, and still be willing to stand up individually for the Lord, regardless of what those around them will think, since they are stuck with being different anyway. Satan has plenty of reasons to try to hold MKs down.

MKs need to specifically denounce any unprotected contact with evil they have had in their past. They need to make it clear to the spiritual world exactly where they stand and cast off any satanic influence in their life in the name of Jesus. Then like Jesus himself, they need to continually be on the alert and ready to rebuke Satan as often and whenever they recognize either his actions or voice. If oppression is suspected, finding a good experienced deliverance minister or counselor is a must.

Child Abuse

Recently, counseling organizations are reporting a high incidence of child abuse in MK's backgrounds. I do not believe that the amount of abuse is high compared to that among people with other backgrounds, but it is high compared with what one might expect from committed Christians. Part of this is because of a belief which has been prominent since the beginning of missions but is now beginning to change—that children and wives are secondary to winning souls.

Many incidents which are being classified as abuse by MK therapists were done by parents and teachers with the best of intentions. The term "abuse" has recently taken on a very broad definition and includes all kinds of mistakes as well as intended harm. That is why I have used quotation marks around this heading. Eight sources of "abuse" are listed here.

1. Neglect - The parents do not understand the implications of decisions they have made on their children. They may react in inappropriate ways during a crisis not having any idea how what they are doing comes across to their children.

   For examples:

   Parents may see that their child is happily adapting to village life and keeping busy, and focus on their work to the exclusion of their children's needs. Taking time and developing close personal relationships with their children may be neglected.

One person tried to shield their child from the death of a village friend, keeping them away from native funeral procedures, not realizing that for the MK child that friendship was very deep, and the need to grieve and to say good bye was intense, even if it would have been fulfilled in a non-western way. They should have looked into the child's perspective.

Parents may be in the jungle facing a major crisis. Perhaps there has been a serious incident involving the people they work with or the church they have planted. This is not known to the MK because the parents have felt it was adult business. If, right then, the child's pet dies or he gets sick, or has some other need, he may have no idea why his parents ignore such a serious event in his life, compared with what else they are dealing with.

2. <u>Cultural</u> - Many things would not be harmful in the culture where they take place, but are very harmful to children of another culture. Another way of looking at this is that some things which severely affect people, are normal in the culture where they are done, but not in missionary culture. In addition to situations regarding the local culture, MKs, being of different culture than dorm parents or house help from other countries, may end up hurt because of this.

Examples:

In some Asian and South American tribal homes children's genitals are sometimes stroked to calm them down and help them go to sleep. Whatever way it affects them, it happens to everyone in that culture and so the outcome fits into that culture. However, should a helper do this to a Western child it might cause harm.

British children in an American children's home may be damaged by what to them would be a dominating, boastful and therefore belittling attitude by the parents. American children would not feel threatened by this, since the parents attitude would not be interpreted by them in that way compared to what they would be used to from home.

3. Emotional and Spiritual Abuse - This is probably the most common kind of abuse. In the isolation of the mission field it is easy for parents to get off on one or more points of theology and impress them on their children without the balance of churches and outside sources. This is especially true in a village situation where isolation can cause "cabin fever" in the family and personal vendettas can get expressed. I cannot comment on the types of abuse that occur here because each family is different.

    However, missionary parents are under tremendous pressure to make sure their kids are Christians for their own reputation. In addition to their concern for their kid's soul, they can resort to manipulation to try to accomplish this.

    The use of religion as punishment: Forcing kids to learn scripture for bad conduct, or making kids go to a Bible study because of their conduct, or screaming verses the child had violated, etc., can give kids a very incorrect

[148]

view of God.

4. <u>Berating and Lack of Love in Dorms</u>

Examples:

Dorm parents sometimes laugh out loud at children's efforts and make fun of what they perceive to be negligence or stupidity. Or they allow children to laugh at one another for the same reason. They don't realize how different families raise their kids, and expect others to be just like their own. Often, they lack the deep sympathy that comes with knowing your own child.

One family may have begun forcing their kids to eat everything on their plate at an early age. Right or wrong, by the age of 7 or 8 their children will be used to it. They may expect it out of all the other 8-year olds in their care, some of whom may never have been forced to eat anything.

Some families insist that there be silence at the table. Others expect discussion. Some families hold hands while they pray, while others insist that hands be in the lap. Some families eat with the left hand, others, with their right. If such differences are not allowed for, children can be treated insensitively.

These are small examples of the types of things which happen over and over in many subtle ways. At a tender age they can be extremely damaging.

One way to avoid a bad situation is for parents to insist on personal private communication with their child. If this is not possible, because the child does not write, or if letters are censored and calls monitored, arrange for the children to communicate through visits with a trusted friend—or better yet, avoid the arrangement entirely and home school the kids. Children must be able to communicate with their parents privately in their absence and must be encouraged to do so. A child who is being abused, even by a foster parent, believes that he deserves it and will usually be too ashamed to report anything.

5. <u>An Army Attitude</u>

    A common form of abuse in boarding situations is the dorm or home which is run like an institution. Children are subjected to a rigorous routine which is meant to meet their needs. Little room is allowed for personal attention. Such homes are often characterized by harsh discipline, limited private outside communication (for example with parents), and an impersonal attitude.

    The basic attitude of the "parents" in such a boarding situation is one of correction and discipline, rather than one of nurture and love. They see children as basically "bad" rather than recognizing that most MKs are in fact very conscientious and need only some guidance of what is expected as well as a lot of love and security. MKs come from Godly homes and have been raised with Godly ideals and aspirations. Their basic need is care, not correction!

6. <u>Sexual Abuse and Beatings</u> - These extreme forms of child abuse occasionally take place. The world is waking up to the temptations on clergy, and the same is unfortunately true for missionaries. Those who do have a problem with

this sort of thing have no place to turn. Because of the tremendous disgrace involved they do not dare to face their problems until it is too late. Or they report it and are automatically let off under the guise of "forgiveness" and allowed to continue.

It would not be fair to create the impression that missionaries in general are prone to abusing their kids in such a manner. They are probably much less likely than any other category of people. Still it is important to note because it does happen, and it is often overlooked or goes unreported because of the overwhelming significance such a report would have. It is significant in light of the fact that the adults in an MK's life, usually other missionaries, are like relatives to him. The nature of the relationship is far more like that of an uncle or a grandparent than it is of neighbor or a friend. Molestation by a dorm parent has the same effect on a child as would incest.

7. <u>Concern for Reputation</u> - Parents concerned with the way their children look to churches can often do a lot of damage. Most MKs remember being pinched at a service between the "It's so wonderful to see you!" and hoarsely whispered to "Just wait until we get to the car!" (Discipline implied). Damage is done when parents are more worried that other people may judge them if their children are prone to excessive emotions or misbehavior, than they are about what may be causing those issues.

8. <u>Peers</u> - Because peers are so influential in MK lives, they can also be sources of abuse. MKs who have grown up with the same older children or peers in boarding schools

for a number of years can develop an inappropriate level of respect for them, usually not accounted for by surrounding adults. If an MK has continually been treated in a negative way by an important peer, this can have as much of an affect as if he was treated badly by his elders. MKs in boarding homes often more or less raise each other, and the way in which this is carried out can positively or negatively affect the person involved in a permanent way. If a child is derided for a fault by other MKs, he may be affected almost as much as if an adult had done the same. A sexual encounter or bullying by a fellow MK may have the same effect as would one between siblings.

Counselors who are looking for sources of rejection in an MK childhood, should look just as closely at the MK's peer relationships as they do at the MK's parental relationships.

Prejudices

Many mission workers continue to treat adult MKs as children long after they have left home. This is true up to approximately age 40. This may seem like an innocent attitude until it is realized that it constitutes a very real prejudice against a group of people who could be a tremendous asset to the mission world. Many MKs complain of being treated as children by co-workers, after returning to the field as missionaries. The difference in treatment is easily noticed as they find that they are treated with respect by those who did not know them as children, but with suspicion by those who did. Many times, MKs have been turned down from missions altogether because they seemed immature in the minds of the evaluators, while others who are younger and much less prepared for overseas work are accepted. This is especially hard on those MKs who, because of boarding situations and separation from home, have been expected to be responsible for themselves for many years even before becoming adults.

I believe the source of this prejudice is not malicious at all, but a natural result of the system by which MKs leave the field at 18. Missionaries never have the chance to watch their own children and other children transform into adults. They leave as kids and are usually never seen again by the whole group. Meanwhile young people that arrive on the field are obviously adults even though they may be only a year or two older than the "children" that just left. A conscious effort must be made to overcome this natural illusion.

Another area where MK adults encounter prejudice is in some church circles. There they may be idealized and expected to be mature above and beyond the normal college-aged person. When the MK fails this expectation by showing some immaturity, disappointment creates subtle resentment, and the church members begin to see the MK as an irresponsible person, rather than realizing that he may be just acting his age.

Another kind of prejudice is encountered when missionaries absorb some of the national prejudices against a local people group and the MK who grows up among them does not. This happens far more often than missionaries would like to admit. The MK is then offended, hurt, or traumatized by actions of the missionaries which are downgrading to the local, which he may identify with.

[153]

I have made a chart which includes the main circumstances which seem to affect MK adjustment in terms of their background, which seems to work in most cases for predicting adjustment to adult life even for non MKs. It covers nurture, trauma, culture, spiritual training and the development of self-esteem. It is very qualitative. You plot your positive or negative degree of each of these aspects on the chart yourself. Then you draw a line between the dots and color all the space between your line and the line across the middle. The amount of space colored above shows how likely you are to succeed compared to the amount colored below the center line. There are two examples including my own.

ADULT MENTAL HEALTH ASSESSMENT

| Nuturing care | Absence of trauma (incl. major culture change) | Communi-ty stability (culture also a factor) | Moral teaching (biblical) | Developing self-esteem and indi-viduality Freedom of opinions | Plot your graph. Connect the dots. Then color in the spaces between your line and the middle line. If most of your color is above the middle line, you are usually healthy. If your graph puts you mostly below the line, you are usually unhealthy.

Suggestion: graph yourself on the chart and see if it matches your life!

This is a tool for understanding how the issues listed can affect someone's life. |
|---|---|---|---|---|---|
| Making kids "tough." Lack of coddling | Possibly wars, deaths, molesta-tion, severe move | Moving and chang-ing friends a lot | Worldly influences | Breaking the will. Molding | |

Example 1 - Pretty normal and even

[154]

ADULT MENTAL HEALTH ASSESSMENT

Nuturing care	Absence of trauma (incl. major culture change)	Communi-ty stability (culture also a factor)	Moral teaching (biblical)	Developing self-esteem and indi-viduality Freedom of opinions	Plot your graph. Con-nect the dots. Then color in the spaces between your line and the middle line. If most of your color is above the middle line, you are usually healthy. If your graph puts you mostly below the line, you are usually unhealthy.
					Suggestion: graph yourself on the chart and see if it matches your life!
Making kids "tough." Lack of coddling	Possibly wars, deaths, molesta-tion, severe move	Moving and chang-ing friends a lot	Worldly influences	Breaking the will. Molding	This is a tool for understanding how the issues listed can affect someone's life.

Example 1 - Me (issues to deal with)

11

Healing in the Midst of Victory

IT SEEMS THAT when the pain is caused by parents answering God's call to the ministry, we are expected not to suffer. We are not allowed to express the hurt. It seems that somehow allowing negative emotions to surface regarding the "devout act", such as having been sent to boarding school, would be walking in Spiritual defeat, rather than victory. It is hard to deal with emotional pain when it was caused by something which we felt was the right thing for someone to have done. People can understand it and are patient when someone has to work through an obviously ungodly infliction of suffering, such as rape by an alcoholic father or rejection from a divorce.

Many MKs have been made to suffer, through separation, being forced to leave their home, and other circumstances. As adults they find that healing is required. Sometimes they are reluctant to pursue healing, feeling that if God cared about their emotions, he wouldn't have meant for the source of the hurt to happen in the first place. Perhaps he didn't. Perhaps he only allowed it. One way or the other, we know that things do happen to Christians which require healing. Everyone knows that Christians doing God's will can get sick. Christians, in the midst of God's will, can get emotionally sick too. It doesn't mean they aren't handling things right; and it doesn't mean God can't use them until they get well.

I have discussed situations which might possibly cause such things as physical, or even emotional and mental, pain or illness. Such conditions would be difficult enough to face under normal circumstances without adding the complex process of culture change. How can an MK know that he is right with God, and be able to sort through new values, when he feels encumbered with a lot of emotional hurt from his past? Does this emotional baggage have to keep him from doing God's will? Not at all!

Whenever you come to a complex problem you have to break it apart and work with one aspect of it at a time. When it is a situation you are going through yourself, you must grab hold of a point of security. You must have an island which you can cling to while you battle the storm raging around you. That point of security can only be Jesus. He is the only one who can carry you through to healing, and keep you whole even while you are on your way there.

The important thing to remember is that you can be an emotional failure—but Spiritually whole! It is foolish to wait for healing of any type before claiming spiritual wholeness. Spirituality is the result of a choice. It is not based on emotion. When we choose Christ, even above ourselves, we can claim all of his promises, even in spite of ourselves. Nevertheless, emotional illness which we are not promised to be free from, may persist. God uses the science He has created sometimes and other times He works more supernaturally or sometimes he just uses it for good.

"God will not give you more than you can bear," is often said by Christians to reassure themselves and others that God will not let you have a nervous breakdown, go insane, or experience unbearable pain. Sadly this is not a promise in the Bible at all. It comes from 1 Corinthians 10:13 as quoted here from the New Living Translation *"13The temptations in your life are no different from what others experience. And God is faithful. He will not allow the temptation to be more than you can stand. When you are tempted, he will show you a way out so that you can endure."* This verse has been taken out of context. It is talking about temptation, not pain. You will never have so much temptation that you have an excuse to sin. We must not judge those who are experiencing unbearable pain or suffering as being Spiritually less mature.

We must embark on the healing process with Christ in the center of our lives just like everything else we do—even if doing so means acknowledging that we don't really know or understand Him yet. There are lots of times when we have to step out in faith by saying "If You are real, I choose You." or

[158]

"If You really love me, then I want You to take charge of my life." This gives God permission to show Himself to be what He claims! This way we are keeping the doors open for Him to do His will.

With Christ in the center of our lives, we <u>know</u> that we are Spiritually whole, because "*… it is no longer I who live, but it is Christ who lives in me …*" Galatians 2:20. It doesn't matter if we are sick physically or emotionally. He can use us in spite of that. It doesn't matter if we have been deeply hurt or rejected, we can go on in spite of that. We can walk into a room full of people and say, "I feel inferior, embarrassed, rejected, no-good, etc., but I know that because it is really Christ who is living in me I am actually a wonderful person despite my feelings." It doesn't matter if a chemical imbalance keeps us depressed. Depression can even be used by God to enable us to weep with those who weep! (You should see how fast the devil flees if the depression was really "oppression" sent from him and we take advantage of it to pray intensely for others who are suffering!)

In fact, the sicker we are emotionally and physically, the more we seem reminded to lean entirely on Him! That is why when Paul talks about his ailment he says:

> "*But to keep me from being puffed up with pride … I was given a painful physical ailment … [8]Three times I prayed to the Lord about this and asked him to take it away. [9]But his answer was: 'My grace is all you need, for my power is greatest when you are weak.' I am most happy, then, to be proud of my weaknesses, in order to feel the protection of Christ's power over me. [10]I am*

content with weaknesses, insults, hardships, persecu-tions, and difficulties for Christ's sake. For when I am weak, then I am strong." 2 Corinthians 12:7-10

We continue to do what we can in order to get well, but while we are doing so, we don't have to get discouraged about, or give up on, our Spiritual life. Our Spiritual life is over and above our emotional and physical life. It doesn't deny it, but it doesn't depend on it either. Our emotions will improve be-cause our Spiritual life is in order. Often, to see this, we have to distinguish between real deep joy and satisfaction, which can go on even in the midst of depression, and the superficial happiness, which can mask deep dissatisfaction. Our Spiritu-al life does not improve because of our emotions; it improves only on the basis of our faith.

Unfortunately, many Christians, believing that we are made whole only by faith, ignore their emotional selves alto-gether. They cover up their feelings. Leaning on God doesn't mean getting rid of feelings, it simply means not letting them run our lives. While such people would never neglect their bodies having realized they had a physical problem, they readily abandon their spirits even while realizing that they have an emotional problem. Emotional problems, or prob-lems of the "soul" or in Greek, "psyche", are part of the suffer-ings of this world just like physical problems.

Once we realize that our real and eternal Spiritual life, is absolutely secure, simply because we have chosen Christ, then we can be free to admit every kind of physical and emo-tional failure. They are all only temporary. We have no need to cover anything up but can be honest and open. We are

[160]

free to feel and express those feelings, and since we are not planning to act on them, we can let them out where we can see them and judge whether they are appropriate or not.

Am I angry at someone? Is it because he is really hurting others, and I ought to be angry? Or is it because he reminds me of someone else who hurt me as a child! Am I feeling inferior? Is it because I am not as good as others in one area? Or, is it because someone has told me I was no good in the past! Do I need to be good at everything? Do I have a concept of God which seems to conflict with what I'm now learning is true? These are thoughts that can make people feel disturbed.

Whenever I realize that one of my thoughts is inappropri-ate, it's time to go to God and ask him for healing. Just exactly like whenever I feel some physical symptom in my body is inappropriate, I go to God for healing. When I do this, God does one of four things: Directs me to a doctor, directs me to a self cure, heals me supernaturally, or has me wait, using the weakness to remind me to lean on Him. This is exact-ly the same for emotional problems, such as inappropriate thoughts or reactions. I go directly to God. He may direct me to a Christian counselor, lead me to a self cure (just realizing where the thought comes from might be enough), perhaps heal me supernaturally, or have me wait, using the weakness to remind me to lean on him or to teach me something in the more lasting spiritual realm.

Realizing that emotional healing and physical healing are the same is important. Scientific studies show that there is very little difference between emotional and mental abnor-malities. More and more doctors are realizing how much our emotions are controlled by our physical state—and how much our physical health is controlled by our emotional state! The whole concept of "mental illness" is getting lost between the two!

Jesus was secure in the knowledge of who he was and where he was going. Yet, he was free to express every range of human emotions. Even to being "sorrowful and troubled" in the Garden of Gethsemane.

Usually it is only by being honest about our feelings, and about where they come from, that we can see the weaknesses that Satan uses to accuse us. When we understand ourselves, it is easier to love ourselves. When we love ourselves, we are not tempted to harm ourselves by engaging in harmful habits. Loving ourselves is absolutely necessary for emotional and mental health. It also helps us to understand and desire to love others more.

One of the biggest areas of emotional pain experienced by adult MKs is the loss of their home, their family, their friends and their culture. Many counselors today talk about the four stages of adjustment to any terrible thing that happens. The four stages are denial, depression, anger and acceptance. Could such a process be Biblical? It reassures me a great deal when I see that Jesus himself went through the exact same stages in regard to the cross. Not only was the cross a traumatic death, but it also meant separation from his Father! Let's look at the four steps one at a time.

The story begins:

"And He took with Him Peter and the two sons of Zebedee, and he began to be sorrowful and deeply dis-

tressed." Matthew 26:37 NKJV [Bold added]

Denial

"... O My Father, if it is possible, let this cup pass from Me; ..." Matthew 26:39 NKJV. Jesus knew the cross had to be endured. He had been saying it for months. It had been predicted since the beginning of history. Yet, here as he worked through the process of grief in the Garden of Gethsemane, he was asking God to change His mind. He simply could not face it! It was just too difficult for his human mind to comprehend. Jesus himself felt free to express his feelings of denial.

Depression

"... My soul is exceedingly sorrowful, even to death ..." Matthew 26:38 NKJV. Sometimes we are afraid that depression itself is a sin. But have we ever been overwhelmed with sorrow "even to death"? That's the kind of depression Jesus felt. Luke, who was a doctor, says that His sweat was as great drops of blood! Luke 22:44 Jesus' depression affected him physically and that was not sin.

Anger

"Then He came to the disciples and found them sleeping, and said to Peter, 'What! Could you not watch with Me one hour?" Matthew 26:40 NKJV. *"... Are you still sleeping and resting? ..."* Matthew 26:45 NKJV

Acceptance

When he met Judas he said, "...' *My friend, go*

ahead and do what you have come for.' ..." Matthew 26:50 NLT. Right away, Jesus' disciples began to defend Jesus, one of them cutting off one of the arresters' ears. Jesus responded to this by saying, *"Put away your sword ..."* Matthew 26:52 NLT

At last Jesus had come to acceptance. His time of sorrow and trouble had accomplished its purpose. Jesus was not afraid to face the reality of his human frailty. He said, *"... The spirit is willing, but the body is weak"* Matthew 26:41 NLT. Yet He persisted in lining up his will with God's. *"... nevertheless, not as I will, but as you will."* Matthew 26:39 NKJV. If we persist in choosing God's will <u>even through</u> our times of sorrow, God will accomplish His will. In the meantime, there's no need to be alarmed by our bodies' very real and natural need to grieve. It does bring us through to healing and acceptance.

Only when we do NOT grieve, turning our anger inward instead of facing it and choosing God's will in spite of it, does it end up doing us damage. It took Jesus one whole night to go from denial to being willing to face the cross. Sometimes it takes us longer. It can even take years. Nevertheless, we have His Spirit in us, so we know that it can be done!

Very often God chooses not to heal us from harmful things that have been done to us until we have been angry enough about them to <u>recognize them as sin</u>. This is so that we will not ever unintentionally hurt others by doing those same things. Many times, I have made the mistake of trying so hard to "forgive and forget," that I missed recognizing the wrong thing that was done for what it was. God wants us to forgive, but not necessarily to forget what happened, since we are to keep on learning the difference between what is loving and what is unloving. This is the only way we can learn from the mistakes of the generation before us. Many people point to where God says, "I will remember your sins no more," and assume that this means one should no longer recall the facts when one forgives. But God forgave David and yet the facts of his sin are written in the Bible to be remembered forever. Instead, I believe he means that he will never hold them against us.

What makes the MK situation more difficult than that of many others, is not that they were hurt, (every human gets hurt), but that because it was all done "in the name of God", they are not allowed to grieve. There is healing and growth in that grieving process. In a sense it is saying, "This is what happened and here is what it did to me." The alternative is to ignore the hurt, and so be unable to truly forgive, to obtain healing, or even learn from the event. In such a case, it can continue to create havoc in your life.

While clinging to the "island" of daily asking Jesus to control our lives, we can be secure about our future and our Spiritual wholeness; and be free to pursue whatever aspects of mental, physical, and emotional ill health come to our attention. Meanwhile we can confidently smile and say; "I may not have it all together, but I have someone in control of my life that does!"

12

Real Success When Cultures Collide

MKs in the World Today

THERE IS AMPLE evidence that MKs are in one of the most advantageous positions in the world regarding their potential. More than children of any other profession, MKs often have opportunities to have a real effect on the world around them. It has been said that one in every 25,000 working class families, one in every 6,000 Baptist Minister's kids, one in every 5,000 lawyer families and one in every 2,500 dentist's kids, produces a child who reaches *Who's Who in America*. But one in every 7 missionary kids reaches *Who's Who.* (Harry Conn, Four Trojan Horses, pg.17-18). This is a phenomenal 357 times as often as any other common profession recorded! The self motivation, learned skills, ability to relate to all kinds of people, and mental and Spiritual maturity of many MKs is unmeasurable. Agnes Sanford, Ann Keimal, Pearl S. Buck, Dr. Charles Leaky, Senator Paul Simon, and Steve Green are all famous MKs.

Just a glance at the prominent MKs in the list above demonstrates the wide variety of lifestyles and professions to which MKs have been able to aspire. Some, such as Ann Keimal and Steve Green, spent their lives busily spreading the Gospel of Jesus Christ. Some of the others are leaders in the secular world. Dr. Leaky is the central figure, other than Darwin himself, in advocating the evolutionary theory of man. They have been Christians, non-Christians and atheists. This demonstrates that it is the upbringing and not necessarily the Spiritual training which gives MKs the potential they have. In fact, their phenomenal potential can be used for good or for bad.

I am certain that many triumphant MKs who are making good use of all of this vast potential are hidden on mission fields or making a positive contribution in secular jobs all over the world, but there are many others—perhaps the majority—who have spent most of their lives just trying to cope with the strange world in which they were not raised. Estimates show that despite the potential of this wonderful upbringing, the suicide, drug, depression and divorce rate for MKs is about the same as for any other group. Indeed, coping with a totally alien world can require all of the wonderful potential which so many MKs have. For many people it would be simply impossible. For some MKs it may seem impossible. Each person's background and inherent skills are different.

The following principles will help break through the barrier which seems to divide "just getting along" from "flying free and high". With Christ we can even go beyond our "potential"

The rest of this chapter is directed towards Adult MKs. However, the principles apply to everyone:

Perceiving Your Background as an Advantage Rather than a Waste

The first step is in realizing that the MK was not created an MK by accident. God had a plan, and that plan included your past. If it was God's will for your parents to be missionaries, it was also for you to be an MK! The Bible says, "*God ... has created us for a life of good deeds which He has already prepared for us to do.*" Ephesians 2:10. I have found great comfort in the words "... he has created us for ..." This means we have never been just a product of circumstances.

Not only did God create us <u>for</u> something, but He is so confident that we will do those things someday that he has already prepared them for us. That means He hasn't said anything like "Uh, Oh, I had something planned for her, but I accidentally planted her in the wrong country!" Actually, scientifically speaking, our upbringing is part of our "creating". Such things as personality, ideology, knowledge, habits, etc., are all either produced or influenced by our upbringing. Therefore, wherever we were raised it is a valid part of the process which God has gone through to create us. God has a plan, and all those things in our background—languages you learned, special abilities, an understanding of the third world, and even boarding schools—are part of it. God had a purpose for every experience He ever allowed you to have, and He can be counted on to see to it that none of it is wasted.

Sometimes as you pour through the materials on choosing a career, or look through the want ads in the newspaper, it's hard to imagine just how your overseas experience relates. In fact, most job applications ask all of the wrong questions. "How many years did you attend school? What was your last place of employment?" They don't ask "How many languages do you speak?" "How good are you at spear-fishing?" "Would you be able to get back on your own if you were dropped off of a bus in the wrong part of a third world city?" You see if you were asked the right questions, you would find that you have all sorts of things to offer the world!

Most MKs are actually overqualified. Imagine a gifted child. He knows how to read and write, but on the first day of school he is tested and asked, "What does this letter say?" "What number is this?" He correctly answers the questions and the teacher knows he is up to the class, but she has no idea where he really belongs. She, too, has asked all of the wrong questions. It makes you want to interrupt and tell the child to volunteer how good he is. The important thing to realize first is that you are overqualified, you're not just a misfit. And that means that those special traits you have can be used, just as soon as they get matched up with the right position.

Here are a few of the valuable traits that many MKs have and some hints as to how they can be useful. All of these are things that the average American just hasn't had the advantage of getting:

[169]

A world perspective - This will benefit any field involving politics, missions, or decisions of any nature. The more accurately you view the world, the better decisions you can make.

An ability to relate inter-culturally - Any job involving people; from Ambassador to home Bible study hostess will benefit from this. Virtually every group in today's mobile world contains people with slightly different cultural backgrounds. You may be the only one in the Sunday school class who befriends the girl from out of state. Or you may become a lawyer and fight for the people who live in the slums.

A broad knowledge and better understanding of facts - When other people are moved to wrong actions by rumors of this or that happening, you may be the only one in your group to understand what's really going on. In any job, the vast array of experience which you have likely had will come in handy as you know much more than just the subject immediately at hand.

A more Biblical set of values - God is the creator and master of the Universe so the more you know about Him, and about the way He says things work, the better off you will be no matter what field you choose!

Sensitivity to people of different backgrounds - If you've had to get along with all types of people all your life, living with them in a foreign country, then you will be able to be sensitive to all kinds of people. This is true even if you have very few experiences similar to theirs. This means you will be able to foster more relationships, and to work more smoothly with other people than most.

An atmosphere of freedom of thought - On a field overseas where everything is quite different from the way books, pastors and teachers say it should be. For example: Suma begging for smoked fish is very different from Dick and Jane throwing the ball. One learns to think independently of the rest of the world. You learn to accept things as they are, not as they should be. If you can lay hold of that and continue to think that way in the U.S., it is one of the secrets of getting through life.

Self-motivation - That's one that _is_ in the want ads! It means that you don't need incentives from others all the time to get work done. If you have a job to do, you do it just because it needs to be done. It's extremely valuable to any job which carries responsibility.

Independence and Individuality - Most MKs have been making most of their own decisions since they were in primary school. Some of them left home at 5 or 6. Others were simply in a safe environment where they were allowed lots of freedom. Those who weren't were in a unique environment where they watched their parents make their own decisions. Very few MKs grew up "just one of the crowd" doing what everyone else does and just trying to fit in. These two traits will carry you ahead in every job. They will enable you to be the leaders.

This list could go on and on. Chances are you aren't going to be able to just march out and convince someone to hire you on the basis of all of these credentials, although, it's certainly worth a try. However, it's important to know that they are there under the surface, and that once you get past the first steps in a career they will probably get noticed. It gives you some idea what to aim at, and it at least gives you a lot of reason not to give up now. 1 Corinthians 15:58 TLB says; " ... *nothing you do for the Lord is wasted* ... " You do realize that you grew up on the mission field "for the Lord"!

The Long Hard Walk

Maybe you're still hurting. Maybe you're feeling too mixed up or "messed up" at this point to get anywhere. Confusion, disillusionment, depression, and homesickness are sapping your energy. Somehow, we've gotten the idea that Christians should never get hurt. We think that if it's God's will it won't affect us. Jesus did God's will, and Jesus had to get away from the crowd to rest and pray. Perhaps you don't see any special characteristics in yourself because compared to others you can barely face your Sunday school, let alone a job.

There is a story that helps me to get perspective about the way we react to stress. Three hikers, John, Tim and Joe, have each just returned from a different trail. They are sitting exhausted in a room. All three are complaining rather miserably. Their backs hurt. There are blisters on their feet, and they're all starving. At last John gets up and fixes supper. He works hard and feels miserable and wonders why none of the others get up and help. A friend comes over and joins in his complaints. "You've both rested just as long as John here, and you haven't lifted a finger to help out! What's the matter with you anyway!" he scolds.

What neither of the scoffers accounted for is how the

paths which the hikers have taken compared. In fact, John only walked 8 miles, while Tim walked 20. John's trail was through shaded woods with gentle slopes. Tim's was rocky and took him up and down hills in the hot sun. No one would probably even guess Joe's problem. He only walked 12 miles, but his legs were shorter and weaker. He can't help that, it was the way he was made. Sometimes we look around at other Christians and think that now that they are in the exact same position as we are, we all ought to be able to do the same things. We forget the effect of the journey behind each, as well as each person's natural strengths and weaknesses.

The process of adjustment to the U.S. from the mission field is especially hard on people who are conscientious. Someone who doesn't care how well he or she does may adjust to the U.S. much easier than someone who wants to do to what is right. People who are conscientious may be better people in the long run, but for a while after returning to the U.S. they may appear to be emotionally weak. Even subtle personality differences can make it much harder for one person than the other. For example: some people tend to process the world around them piece by piece. Each piece of information builds on something they already know. They are unlike people who grab on to all sorts of new ideas at once. When everything changes suddenly, it is especially hard for such people to adapt. It may take years to gather the amount of information over again in order for them to perform seemingly simple actions, such as being friendly at a party. Others just accept things however they come. They do what they see others doing even if it doesn't make sense. The world needs both kinds of people equally much, but it's easier for the second type to adapt.

Some fields are more difficult to adjust from than others. Some people had the right kind of nurture from their parents. Others' parents may have been better in other areas which did not particularly help with adjustment. Some MKs went to the field as children, some in their teens, and some went only for a year or two. It is unfair to compare all of these people together and expect them all to adjust, or be able to smoothly function in the same length of time. It is even worse to try to compare them with people who have been in the U.S. all along—to treat them as if they had never gone through the trauma that they did.

Just as it took time and a healing process to bring the hikers back to normal functioning levels after their various hiking experiences, it takes time and a healing process to bring MKs back to normal functioning levels after their various transition and separation experiences.

Lots of MKs and people who work with MKs have made statements like, "Well, you've been back for two years. You ought to be over all those hurts by now!" Then the MK feels forced to deny what is fact, and inside he becomes angry at his feelings. If it still hurts, it still hurts. There is nothing we can do about that. What we can do is go on in spite of it! We can go on, trusting Jesus to keep healing as time goes by, recognizing that when it is all over we will have become better.

Another thing we tend to do is instead of forgiving as is necessary for healing, we try to pretend we aren't really angry. That's why the Bible says, "... *be angry and do not sin ...*"

[174]

Ephesians 4:26 NKJV. The feeling of anger itself is not a sin! The only problem is that it can cause us to sin. It sure is better to admit it is there and keep an eye on it while you're overcoming it, than to try to cover it up where it might indeed cause sin.

The only way I know to really get rid of anger is to forgive, and the only way I know to forgive is to ask God to forgive. If you ask God to forgive someone, not to hold their sin against them, you will find that you have forgiven them. Try it! It works every time. If you can't ask God to forgive them yet, then start by asking him to help you!

I believe there are two kinds of forgiveness: Spiritual forgiveness, which can be done immediately by a choice of the will, and emotional forgiveness, which can take a long time. The important thing is Spiritual forgiveness. The feelings will follow as they are properly expressed.

One other thing you can do when you hurt is specifically ask God to heal those wounds. If he can heal physically, even through doctors, then he can surely heal emotionally. If he doesn't, that's OK too. He doesn't promise to heal emotions any more than cancer, but he promises to work them out for good. *"And we know that all things work together for good to those who love God, to those who are the called according to His purpose."* Romans 8:28 NKJV. *"And this small and temporary trouble we suffer will bring us a tremendous and eternal glory, much greater than the trouble."* 2 Corinthians 4:17

Releasing Yourself from The Strings of Various Cultures

Probably the thing which hinders MKs from reaching their

potential more than anything else is the many cultures they may still be tied to. They are tied to the past, because they can't just throw out everything they have ever been taught is right. They are tied to the present because they don't want to offend everyone around them. They are tied to cultures they have met with along the way because these had some good ideas. At some point, however, all of these cultures are going to clash, or at the very least become too much to follow. They become a burden to hold you down.

Culture is nothing more than a language. It is an agreement by which we understand each other. If I say, "I appreciate you," you would understand what I meant because you speak English. If I went to a meeting on time every time, the Americans at the meeting would "understand" that I was enthusiastic and serious about the meeting. Whether I meant it or not, that is what I would be saying. If someone burps after a meal in Arabia, he is saying "Thank you. That was delicious!" If someone burps after a meal in a Western home, he is showing disrespect. If company comes over to your house, and you live in South America (or for that matter in Middle Ages England), you will apologize for your "meager surroundings." "I am only a poor peasant and I have no food," you will say as you proceed to offer a meal. This will mean that you are honored to have them as a guest and that you consider them wonderful company. If you said the same thing in the U.S., it might mean that you are dishonestly looking for a handout, and that you see your guest only as someone from whom you might benefit financially. Or, it might indicate that you have a poor self image and a negative outlook on life.

[176]

If culture is only a language, then all that matters is that I communicate what I want to communicate. If I was in a market in a country where they do not speak English, I would not say "I would like to buy those potatoes". I would know that this would not communicate what I want to say. I would try to say it in the language of the person to whom I was speaking. If I did not know that language, I might say it in English, but I would back it up with every other form of communication I knew (e.g., hand signals), recognizing that they might misunderstand me and being patient with them if they did not. This is exactly how we should treat culture. If you can say it, or rather do it, the way the people around you do it, then do so. If not, do it your way, and back it up with other communication such as speaking, or signs. Smile! Explain that you are doing this to mean whatever it is you want to show. Then if they still do not understand, be patient with them. Meanwhile keep trying to learn their language.

This is where it helps to try to say things literally. Get used to saying to people exactly what you mean in literal words, and you will find you are communicating what you want to communicate more often. It is hard to believe how often we humans speak using hints, hidden meanings, and obscure body language. Some experts believe that 80% of what we say is "non verbal". Also, ask others to tell you what they are hearing you say in their own words, whenever you can, just to be sure that they understand what you mean. You can even repeat things they have said in your own words frequently, which will make them feel that you really cared enough to listen. It will also help you learn to perceive their hidden language symbols more correctly.

Jesus said that loving one another, plus God, summed up all of the commands. Basically, this was what God had been trying to say all along; but people didn't know what love was, so he gave us ten (and more) examples. As Christians our real goal is to be loving. We can be free to choose any culture we want to as long as we are doing what is loving. This means if it makes no difference to anybody else, I'll act the way I'm most comfortable; but if that might offend you then I'll try to act differently for your sake. *"For you have been called to live in freedom, my brothers and sisters. But don't use your freedom to satisfy your sinful nature. Instead, use your freedom to serve one another in love."* Galatians 5:13 NLT

Here is another example. The MK guy wants to say, "I am cool". So, he keeps his hair long and goes barefoot. Instead of hearing "I am cool," what others hear is "I am a bum." That's OK if that's what he wants to go around saying. If it's not, then he ought to wear designer clothes. That will say "I am cool" to Americans.

Should you go to the family reunion? Ask yourself, "What will it say to my relatives if I don't?" Maybe you don't think it is important, but if not going will communicate to them that you don't want to have anything to do with them, is that really what you want to say right now? Should you choose a high-paying job, over another one which will help people? The American way would be to take the high paying one. What will it say if I don't? It will say that I am a little irresponsible. (Some Americans consider making money the most responsible thing you can do.) What will be the most loving?

[178]

Helping people. Maybe it's time to risk looking irresponsible in order to do what communicates God's love to others by helping people. That's what we're really here on earth for.

You can pick and choose your own culture however and whenever you like. Wear designer clothes one day and hand-me-downs the next. Do whatever you like, but ask yourself "Am I communicating what I want to communicate?" and "Am I doing what is the most loving?"

America - "Land of Freedom"

"Freedom?" When I first came back from the mission field I resented that word! They said America meant freedom, and I felt like it was prison. I had never been so restricted or heard of so many rules in my life. Everything I thought of, it seemed, was something you couldn't or shouldn't do.

I couldn't go for a walk very far by myself. It wasn't safe to go somewhere without telling someone. I wasn't supposed to just drop by homes without calling. When I called they were always busy. None of the activities that I wanted to do existed, and all the activities that were available cost money. I wasn't supposed to hang around with certain people at school, I <u>was</u> supposed to hang around the kids at church. Perhaps it would have been easier for a guy, or perhaps it might have seemed free to an MK from a restrictive field, but for me it was really a prison. I couldn't see beyond the walls.

Two years later my husband and I moved to Europe. It was lovely. The air was cleaner, relationships seemed to be more natural, and so was the lifestyle. It wasn't long, however, before we discovered what those who called America "free" knew all along. There was only one way of doing things. It seemed to be a "better" way than ours, as was the opinion of our European relatives, and it was the only way. Buying a house, getting a job, and moving all required the notification, and often permission of the government. Everything had to be done "right". Rigid standards guarded everything from pet care to choosing a doctor. Even the culture itself was restrictive. Natural indeed, but there was only one way of doing things—and that had to be learned in order to fit in with society at all.

In the United States you can be any way you want to be. This is certainly not the only country in the world where people can be anything they choose to be, but it is one of the few. In many of the countries where MKs grew up, they had the freedom to do practically anything their minds could think of. However, their parents had to apply for extensive permission for their particular jobs, as well as to live there. The fact is most MKs return to the U.S. because there is no place for them on the field as adults.

In the United States you can start any business, choose any career, and seek any lifestyle. Of course, you must live with the consequences of what you choose. But the choice is there. About the only things which are actually forbidden by law in the U.S. are those things which are harmful to one's self or others. There are many wonderful lifestyles in many countries around the world. But in the U.S., you can choose any lifestyle. You can be yourself.

Most of the restrictions I experienced when I first arrived in the U.S., were restrictions held up by the particular people

I was with. I could have chosen to stay with a different group. They might not have been as healthy, but it was my choice not to. At that time, I didn't realize that I had that choice. If I had, I would not have felt that I was in a jail. I would have realized instead, that people were only trying to take care of me.

Making use of that freedom is another issue. What most States-siders take for granted, and don't know how to convey to MKs, is: 1) how to use that freedom; and 2) what to do when you want to break out of the realm of average. Many MKs see other Americans doing things out of the ordinary and getting away with it, while when they themselves try it they are told it would never work. The MK doesn't realize that the State-sider probably got the same response when he first started but he ignored it. For example, when my brothers first announced that they wanted to walk from Canada to Mexico, my relatives responded with alarm and disgust. They told them it was a waste of time and money, and that they would never be able to make it. Yet when they actually did it, they were touted as heroes! One man in the U.S. even became nationally famous by doing a similar thing.

This is the pattern that exists in most parts of the United States. If you say you want to, or are capable of living a different lifestyle or doing something different, people will start by opposing you. Then if and when you are successful, you are praised and admired! If you fail, the matter is quietly forgotten, unlike some societies where you would thereafter be remembered as foolish. That is the American way; taking risks and being responsible for the risks you take. That is freedom!

Letting God Adapt You to the Perfect Lifestyle for You

Even with all the advice in the world on culture, with all the choices on hand, it can all get mighty confusing. With absolutely the very best intentions we still don't really know what the best niche is for us. We might research our every action and still choose the wrong ones for what God has called us to do. We might, that is, if it weren't for Him. Fortunately, He has His hand in all of this. It's not our responsibility to develop our lives, it's His. All we have to do is obey what we know! This is because we are His kids.

When my son was three, he woke up with a terrible nightmare. He dreamed that some important men demanded that he sign his name on some papers, but he did not yet know how to write! What a terrible burden for my child, to believe that he must be responsible for that which he had not yet been taught. God does not want that burden on us either. He promises to handle the teaching—we are only responsible for what we know. We can't sin accidentally!

MKs tend to feel a lot of guilt because they are almost always in a state of doing something that somebody they respect somewhere says is wrong. It is important to differentiate between what "somebody somewhere" says, and what "I know." *"Therefore, to him that knoweth to do good, and doeth it not; to him it is sin."* James 4:17 KJV. We sin by choosing to go against what we know. And it's up to God to make sure we know the right things. Each of us is on a journey and God teaches us what is right as we go.

There are so many verses showing that God is taking the responsibility for developing us along the right paths that it

[182]

is hard even to know where to begin!

> *"And I am sure that God who began the good work within you will keep right on helping you grow in his grace until his task within you is finally finished on that day when Jesus Christ returns"* Philippians 1:6 TLB

> *"To Him who is able to keep you from falling and to bring you faultless and joyful before his glorious presence"* Jude 1:24

> *"... As long as His Spirit remains in you, you do not need anyone to teach you. For his Spirit teaches you about everything, and what he teaches is true, not false ..."* 1 John 2:27

> *"When the Spirit of truth comes, he will guide you into all the truth ..."* John 16:13 NLT

God wants us to do what is right even more than we do. He can see to it that we know the things He wants us to know, and He can enable us to do them. The only place we come in is in the choosing. That is the one thing that God gave man—the right to our own will. He will not take over our lives unless we give Him permission. He will not cause us to do His will, unless that is what we would choose. That's exactly what it means to "die daily." It is not some mystical, agonizing thing. It is simply saying to God: "No matter what the outcome is, no matter what the path will be like, I want You to be in charge of my life. The responsibility is Yours."

> *"From now on, then, you must live the rest of your earthly lives controlled by God's will and not by human desires."* 1 Peter 4:2

There are three wonderful things that God will do in that process, with our permission only.

<u>A new creature</u> - He will make me into a whole new creature. What wonderful implications this has for the MK. God isn't done with us yet. He is making us into a new creature, "... *by the renewing of your mind ...*" Romans 12:2 KJV, so that we will exactly fit wherever we are to end up!

<u>A place in the body</u> - We will have a place in the body of Christ. We are going to fit in. "*He is the one who holds the whole building together and makes it grow into a sacred temple dedicated to the Lord. ²²In union with Him you too are being built <u>together with all the others into a place</u> where God lives through his Spirit.*" Ephesians 2:21,22. It's part of His plan to make us a functional part of the church. We won't be left to the side because nobody understands us, and we don't understand them.

<u>Righteousness</u> - We don't even have to wait for this one. Because of God's mighty plan of forgiveness, we are already righteous. "*God made him who had no sin to be sin for us, so that in him <u>we might become the righteousness of God</u>.*" 2 Corinthians 5:21 NIV

We can count on being able to always do what we know is right for us! While other people have to struggle to do what is right, we Christians have only to claim Christ's power, because he promises that He is able to keep us from sinning. "*because God is always at work within you making you willing and <u>able to obey his own purpose</u>.*" Philippians 2:13, "*To him who is able <u>to keep you from falling</u> and to bring you faultless*

[184]

..." Jude 1:24, "... *'My grace is all you need, ...*" 2 Corinthians 12:9, etc.

Living a Righteous Life in the Midst of Cultural Collisions

I believe there is only one way to live a righteous life in the middle of so many culturally different ethics and values. This is a provision from God, an aspect of His grace, so necessary for this kind of problem. It is the only method I know by which someone can cope with major culture and value changes. I believe it is a principle so valuable to daily life, that it is worth all of the cultural struggles I have been through to have learned it. Here it is:

God gave man his own will. That's why we have so many decisions to make in the first place. If it weren't for our own will we would be just like animals, doing whatever came to mind. Instead, we are responsible to make choices in everything we do. Fair enough, now comes the exciting part. We can give our wills back to God! That makes Him in control of what we do. It sounds incredible, but it's Biblical. Of course, it is our nature to want to control things, so we naturally keep on taking things back into our own hands. In fact, we do so almost daily. But any time we are not sure how to act, all we need to do is to consciously give our will back to Him and He will take over! Romans 13:14 NLT "*But let the Lord Jesus Christ take control of you, and don't think of ways to indulge your evil desires.*"

People worry about God taking our will away when He takes control, but he doesn't do that. His Spirit joins with our spirit to make it wonderful! He created us in His image and loves to watch us create and choose things, but he guides us as a loving father. Even Jesus said, "*I can of Myself do nothing ...*" John 5:30 NKJV. Jesus also said, "*Take my yoke upon you and learn from Me, for I am gentle and lowly in heart, and you will find rest for your souls. *[30]* For My yoke is easy and My burden is light*." Mathew 11:29-30 NKJV. He is telling us that when we are connected to him as a yoke connects two bulls, he will lead us along together with Him. He will not eliminate us.

If God is in charge of our will, He will lead us into what is truly loving, without our having to understand the details. If God is in charge of our will, He will do whatever is culturally necessary. When God is in charge, He will see to it that our talents and uniqueness are used for the good of mankind. When God is in charge, He will make sure we don't over step our limits. He knows them better than we do. When God is in charge everything is guaranteed to come out right! So just sit back and relax, enjoy life, the Boss has everything under control. What a relief. It takes all the burden out of everything. Now you can do whatever you feel is right, without being afraid of your mistakes, or of neglecting to use your skills. You can trust that whatever it is you are doing, God is working it out for good. After all, when we give our will over to God, its "*... no longer I who live, but it is Christ who lives in me ...*" Galatians 2:20

> "<u>*Whoever has the Spirit, however, is able to judge the value of everything*</u>*, but no one is able to judge him. As the scripture says, 'Who knows the mind of the Lord? Who is able to give him advice?' <u>We, however, have the mind of Christ</u>*." 1 Corinthians 2:15,16

[186]

"But God has brought you into <u>union with Christ Je-sus</u>, and God has <u>made Christ to be our wisdom</u>. By him we are put right with God; <u>we become God's holy people</u> and are set free. ³¹So then, as the scripture says, 'whoever wants to boast must boast of what the Lord has done.'" 1 Corinthians 1:30, 31

"But as for you, Christ has poured out his Spirit on you. <u>As long as his Spirit remains in you, you do not need anyone to teach you. For his Spirit teaches you about everything, and what he teaches is true, not false</u> ..." 1 John 2:27

I picture it like this. If I take a three year old to the park, I will be in "control" of him just by the responsibility of taking him there and watching over him. But I will enjoy him as he chooses what to play on and how to do so. As he slides down the slide, or makes castles in the sand box, I will laugh with him and enjoy his every move and choice. I will gladly push him on the swings if he chooses to do that. But if he tries to eat sand or goes over to an ant pile, I will stop him immediately. I will decide when it is time for him to come home and will enforce it. I am in control. We are to be like children.

God wants to teach each of us individually just exactly how He wants us to live our lives by living His very own life through us in the form of the Holy Spirit. He is the one responsible to teach us right from wrong.

Does this mean we are perfect? No. We still have a lot of growing to do. But we can be righteous. I see it like this. A little tree may not bear blossoms or fruit but the gardener delights in how it is just growing there, four or five feet tall. It is whole and right as it is, even though it is small and seemingly insignificant in the garden and has lots of growing to do.

About Mistakes

Mistakes must be clearly understood by anyone in a multi-cultural position, since virtually anything they may do might look like a mistake to someone of a different subculture. Satan loves to use mistakes as opportunities to accuse people of sin. We must differentiate between mistakes and willful disobedience. When we willfully sin we know we may have to endure the consequences. When we make mistakes, even while trying to do things in our own strength, that is without wanting Christ in control, there is no sin involved. When we have chosen Christ's control, we <u>know</u> we are called according to His purposes, so we know that our "mistakes" will be used for good.

Often, I find God allows me to make a mistake where it doesn't do any harm, so that I know what to avoid later where it really would do harm. Other times God uses my "mistakes" to accomplish those things which are over and above my best human judgment. Sometimes He does both at once.

This principle that God uses our mistakes, is a concrete demonstration of God's "power in our weakness," and "wisdom in our foolishness". It actually occurs so often that many examples could be used. One example occurred when my husband felt that we should take a substantial risk to our finances and borrow enough money to import a car from Europe, which we thought we could sell for more in the United States. We asked God to have <u>His way</u> in the matter, and

[188]

of course we did all of the research we could, even checking into the safety requirements of car manufacturers in the U.S. Used Volkswagen Beetles seemed to be the safest small transaction, and Rob's brother in Holland quickly found one in our price range. It was a very un-American hand-painted bright pea-green and orange, and would need paint, but was otherwise in fine shape.

When we finally received our VW bug and began to modify it for the United States, we discovered one little aspect of the rear body structure which was impossible to modify. We had just learned about the principle of "putting on the mind of Christ," choosing His will, and then stepping out and doing what we thought best. This was a real test. Our friends insisted we had failed, and God could not be trusted to make this right.

Our only choice was exporting the car to Mexico, and we soon discovered there was a law forbidding the sale of cars exported to Mexico. We would have to give it away. We called a small group of businessmen with a non-profit organization giving goods to needy people across the border and learned that there was a definite need for a car. When we reached the home of the pastor to whom the car was to be given, we were surprised to notice that he could not stop crying. When we asked for an interpreter, he told us "Not only did God answer my highest prayers these last two years for a car, but he even picked the color I had asked for!" We didn't know whether to laugh or to join in the tears! Later we learned that he had been walking 12 and sometimes 20 miles three times per week, as the only pastor serving three churches!

Rob and I don't believe for one minute that this was a mistake out of God's will. That pastor needed a car. Getting one for him was nothing short of a miracle. Yet God chose to provide through us the exact answer to his prayers, right down to the unusual color. We believe God led us into that "mistake." We also learned from it and have been even more cautious about importing since then. We eventually ended up getting all that we had paid on that car in income tax later when we really needed the money.

God has worked this same way for us many times since then. It is always so amazing to look back and see the difference between the mistakes we make on our own, and the "mistakes" we make when we have chosen God's will. We must be confident that when we "let God transform us inwardly", letting Him live His life through us, we will be able to "know the will of God" and to make accurate value judgments. We will be able to do what is right, even if we don't yet truly understand the culture we are working in. God will be guiding our every move. When you know how complex cultures are, and how easy it is to go wrong in them, you realize that believing this requires believing in the supernatural power of God to work in and through the most minute details of our lives. Paul knew this when he said:

> "so that it is no longer I who live, but it is Christ who lives in me. This life that I live now, I live by faith in the Son of God, who loved me and gave His life for me."
> Galatians 2:20

He echoed it again when he said:

> "There is nothing in us that allows us to claim that we

are capable of doing this work. The capacity we have comes from God;" 2 Corinthians 3:5

Even though we can let God be in charge of letting us know what values we should follow, a knowledge of the culture of the people we are working in, can be a tool in His hands towards that goal. Such knowledge can be gained by the principles of cross-cultural communication, such as honesty and "literal language," and by an openness to the kinds of differences set out as examples in previous chapters. God, who designed the world in the first place, and knows the ins and outs of every culture, always wants us to increase in knowledge. He uses and even guides our mistakes when we let him, but He never wants us to make mistakes on purpose. Just as He promises to provide for our financial needs but still expects us to work, so He promises to guide us in the value choices we make, but still expects us to find out all we can about the culture of the people we are with.

Real Success in Life

What is success? This is an important question. To be honest most of us MKs feel, if we were asked, that success is doing things well and adjusting well. As MKs we often think we have settled the whole issue because we <u>know</u> that it isn't money, as even American teachers emphasis whenever the subject comes up. In fact, they often confirm the MK culture definition, without realizing that it also is not the true answer. If we were very sure of being well-adjusted and doing a good job in our field, we would probably feel that we had attained success. I have asked MKs in crisis, "What should God do to make you feel that He is in control of your life?" Usually they want to feel that they are adjusting well to the U.S. (or school or whatever), and that they are doing a good job at what they are called to do. But is this the Bible definition of success?

Jesus said, "*You will be expelled from the synagogues [churches], and the time will come when those who kill you will think that by doing this they are serving God. ³People will do these things to you because they have not known either the Father or me.*" John 16:2,3. Being kicked out of church and killed?! This does not sound like adjusting well to society to me!

Paul could have gotten out of jail, but he had appealed to the emperor. One lousy mistake! If only he had known. Paul thought he was called to evangelize the world, instead he was stuck in prison writing letters because of one lousy "mistake". I think that's why he later wrote that he was a "... *prisoner of Christ Jesus ...*" Ephesians 3:1. He knew Christ could have gotten him out of there. He trusted that God must have had him in jail for a purpose. But would he have felt that he was "doing his job well"? Paul never knew the long-term results of the letters he had to write because he could not go to the churches in person.

So, what is success according to the God who made us? Jesus said, "*If you obey my commands, you will remain in my love, just as I have obeyed my Father's commands and remain in his love. ¹¹I have told you this so that my joy may be in you and that your joy may be complete. ¹²My commandment is this: love one another, just as I love you.*" John 15:10-12. Success **is obeying god and loving one another**! It is being able to do the right things! It is doing the Father's will. Jesus was

[192]

not well known as a carpenter, which was his job. He didn't have a stable home, and he was not "well-adjusted" because most people in authority misunderstood him and hated him. But he obeyed God. That is what is important.

There are lots of verses which tell us that He does enable us to do what is right. Not in some distant future, but right now. He does this as often as we let Him.

"*I can do all things* through Christ who strengthens me." Philippians 4:13 NKJV

"… *Those who live as the Spirit tells them to have their minds controlled by what the Spirit wants.*" Romans 8:5

"… *The capacity we have comes from God; ⁶it is he who made us capable of serving the new covenant* …" 2 Corinthians 3:5,6

"*For our love for God means that we obey his commands. And his commands are not too hard for us, ⁴because every child of God is able to defeat the world* …" 1 John 5:3,4

Even in the old Testament it says,

"*Give yourself to the Lord; trust in him, and he will help you; ⁶he will make your righteousness shine like the noonday sun.*" Psalm 37:5,6

Sure, we ourselves cannot withstand temptation, but He is always there to help us! Instead of being impossible, this is the only form of success which is possible for anyone to obtain, whatever their circumstances. "*Happy are those whose greatest desire is to do what God requires; God will satisfy them fully!"* Matthew 5:6. He says if this is your goal, you will be completely satisfied! All we have to do is give Him permission to take over and it will be done.

The one thing you can be sure of, whether you ever succeed in the world's eyes or not, is that you can succeed in God's eyes. By His promised and ever available power, of course. In fact, when you let Jesus control your life it is impossible to fail. Imagine it! "... *in union with Christ we are always led by God as prisoners in Christ's victory procession* ..." 2 Corinthians 2:14. Prisoners in a celebration of real **success**— even when cultures collide!

THE END

WORKING EXAMPLES

Typical MK Ethics And Values,
And The Complications They May Cause

This section contains examples of MK cultural differences, and ways people react when their culture conflicts with others around them. Since every MK comes from a different background, some of these might not apply to some MKs. They are to be used only as examples of the types of things that may make up differences between MK culture (especially from the third world) and North American or "State-side" culture.

WORK

Work Must Accomplish A Goal Or Fill A Need. Money is not an acceptable motivation to work.

Explanation of MK value

This value is wide spread, but usually held at the subconscious level. Some MKs believe this way openly. Others are easily talked into accepting money as a motivation on the surface while underneath they may never be satisfied with just working for money. Following are a few factors which might lead an MK to hold this value:

(a) The work of the children's missionary parents is not related to income whatsoever. As long as the missionary's job is maintained, he is supported. Diligence is produced by other forms of motivation.

(b) On the field jobs are often passed freely from one person to another according to the needs of the branch. Satisfaction comes from filling a need, not from doing a certain type of work or just having a job. Often the workers are not paid. Even non-Christians in third-world countries are often working to fill needs rather than to obtain a particular salary.

(c) The "good" adults which some young MKs see are all missionaries who don't work for money. Expatriates who do work for money are often implied by missionaries to be "bad". Since such a child may not be told about drinking, infidelity, cheating, or other reasons the expatriate might indeed be bad—working for money may be the only thing he sees is different about the expatriate.

(d) The Bible: Jesus himself never earned money but worked very hard. "*Seek ye first the Kingdom of God, and his righteousness; and all these things shall be added unto you.*" Matthew 6:33 KJV. How can selling brushes be seeking first the Kingdom of God?

Possible Complications

(a) An MK may be very reluctant to solicit for a job. "If someone needs me, why don't they ask for me" is a subconscious feeling behind this.

(b) MKs with this value may accept jobs for which they are underpaid, such as volunteer work, while other jobs might be available which would seem to be better opportunities to a States-sider. For example, one might work after school at a church nursery, while refusing a thriving sales job. A few MKs may feel uncomfortable seeking a paying job if there are other needs at home which appear to demand their labor more.

(c) An MK who holds this value subconsciously may be deeply unsatisfied with a job even though it is regular, comfortable and well paying; if he feels it is not filling a genuine community need. This particularly applies to sales jobs.

Occupations Must Involve Helping People

<u>Explanation of MK value</u>

This value is fairly common among most MKs, including those who have spent much time in the U.S. It is held quite strongly even when only on a subconscious level.

(a) All of the occupations which the MK sees on some fields either involve helping people or hurting people. In third world countries there are usually businessmen who take advantage of the poor; and doctors, missionaries, ambassadors, or priests, etc. who help the poor.

(b) Missionaries strongly teach the need to serve the Lord in missions or other helping vocations. In addition to the MK's own training in this area, he will have heard his parents make appeals to churches for altruistic work over and over again. Other values, such as the high priority of relationships over money, support this value.

This is the reason so many MKs become such things as doctors, social workers, missionaries, teachers, nurses, or join the armed forces. This value provides tremendous motivation to pursue such honorable occupations with zeal.

Possible Complications

(a) MKs may say there are no career openings available to them when actually there are career openings, but they don't involve helping people.

(b) MKs may take a job which does not involve helping people, only to find it extremely dissatisfying.

Putting One's Abilities Down - A Very Important Aspect of Work Relationships.

States-side Opposite: States-siders build their abilities up in the eyes of those in authority over them.

Explanation of MK value

The source of this value is the culture of South-East Asian countries. Other third-world countries may do this too.

Possible Complications

If this trait is not recognized as a cultural method of communication, it will be believed. The boss will believe the MK is as bad as he or she says they are. This could mean the loss of a job, or at least lack of advancement. Sometimes if a states-side boss has enough evidence that the MK is not as inferior as he lets on, he will decide that he has a low self esteem. Either way, this is greatly in conflict with the States-side way of "selling one's self".

A Person's Attire Says Nothing About His Work Character

States-side Opposite: Many States-siders subconsciously

tend to evaluate people by their economic status. They look at clothes, cars, education, etc. when making a first impression decision as to what kind of character the person has. In a country where people with good characteristics, such as diligence, determination, and honesty, usually can get ahead financially, this makes sense.

Explanation of MK value

(a) MKs get to know people closely, from a wide variety of economic levels, and find no difference in character. In the third world, honest, hard-working, conscientious individuals do not necessarily get ahead of others financially, depending upon the country.

(b) The MK himself will not fit into any particular economic bracket. He will have the privileges of some as well as the lack of others. For example, he may go to a private school, and wear second-hand clothes.

(c) Bible verses:

"Suppose a rich man wearing a gold ring and fine clothes comes to your meeting, and a poor man in ragged clothes also comes. ³If you show more respect to the well-dressed man and say to him, 'Have this best seat here,' but say to the poor man, 'Stand over there, or sit here on the floor by my feet,' ⁴then you are guilty of creating distinctions among yourselves and of making judgments based on evil motives." James 2:2-4

"Listen, my dear friends! God chose the poor people of this world to be rich in faith and to possess the kingdom which he promised to those who love him." James 2:5

Also reference to the fact that Jesus was poor.

Complications in U.S. Culture

(a) An MK may see no reason to wear a certain type of clothes or drive a certain type of car in order to look like a certain type of person. He may deliberately dress poorly, depending on his own taste. If he chooses to dress like someone from a poorer economic bracket than his church, job, or school, he may be severely misjudged as to his own character. Some have lost their jobs because they refused to project the "right image".

(b) Since he sees no value in a certain type of appearance, he may judge those who do, finding their efforts wasteful or based on vain motives.

(c) He or she may freely choose to associate with some rich and some poor people. In this country where there is a certain amount of truth to the notion that those who work hard and have good values get ahead, this habit may cause him to latch on to some bad company.

MONEY

Money Does Not Mix With Recreation Or Friendship

Explanation of MK value

(a) On the field everyone typically has just enough to get by. Therefore, out of kindness to each other's position, missionaries never charge each other for services except when absolutely necessary.

(b) Recreation on a remote field is always free. Beaches, the jungle, camp outs, hiking, sports (usually volley ball or soccer) are always free. Recreation is also social, and friends would never expect money from each other.

Note: Exceptions to this are when absolutely necessary, at which time the exact minimum figure is calculated and requested from participants only as able. For example, the need for gas.

Complication in U.S. Culture

(a) MKs may be offended when youth groups or Sunday Schools and churches plan retreats or even evening outings, and require payment in order to attend.
(b) An MK who cannot afford a certain group outing may come anyway, and may offend their host by being "unable" to contribute their share.
(c) MKs may be uncomfortable with park fees, and will therefore choose a public access to some natural resource instead, thereby missing some of this country's best-kept natural resources.
(d) MKs may shun sports such as bowling, skating, golf, and racquetball because of fees, and will therefor miss out on good sources for both recreation and relationships.
(e) MKs may be offended when friends or neighbors have parties during which they try to sell them products such as Amway, or Mary Kay Cosmetics, or other items where the seller has something to gain personally from the sale (virtually all sales.)

Money Should Never Be Used For Personal Satisfaction

Explanation of MK value

(a) Parents, conscientious of the meaning behind financial support, teach that their income is to be used for their needs and not for personal satisfaction in any way.

(b) On the field, very little money is used. It does not become associated with fun things, like a trip to an amusement park or a toy bought by grandma at the store. Very few examples will be found among missionaries of people spending money on themselves.

(c) The types of things available in stores in third world countries mostly concern necessities such as rice, lanterns and soap. An occasional ball or fishing rod may be the only attraction for a child. When there are toys, they are often grossly overpriced, so that parents are more likely to rely on packages from grandparents to supply their kids with things. This removes the connection with money entirely.

(d) MKs find plenty to do without money, and personal satisfaction is found in climbing trees, hunting, riding bikes, exotic pets, swimming, tubing, jungle trips, etc.

Complications in the U.S.

Many MKs feel guilty for all the things they do for themselves which involve money. Since everything you do in the U.S. involves money, this can have severe and far reaching consequences:

(a) The constant use of money may add to the vague sense of guilt MKs carry around with them. This habit may be so far removed from the world which they came from.

(b) MKs will usually be extremely cautious about buying

anything for themselves. Note: Sometimes the opposite occurs. Compulsive buying. This could be a temporary over-reaction to the change in circumstances. It does not happen very often.

(c) Simple decisions about budget can become rather strenuous, since even with a cautious approach, little experience may have been had with regard to using finances for pleasure.

(d) This can be a source of tension within marriages (MK to non-MK).

(e) Since most stress reducing activities in the U.S. involve spending money on yourself in some way such as shopping, recreation, snacks, hobbies etc., an MK may be limited in his own stress-reducing methods rather severely, causing stress to compound.

(f) MKs needing help may refuse to spend money if it is for themselves only, for example for counseling, or a trip back home.

SUCCESS

The Definition Of Success (Self-Worth) Is Excellence

States-side opposite: Success is Money and Lifestyle—"The American Dream."

<u>Explanation of MK value</u>

(a) Parents are highly educated and strive for perfection in their work. The nature of Bible translation requires this thinking; naturally it must be done right or not at all.

(b) Fields with British influence will reflect some of the British value on excellence.

(c) Parents and teachers are aware that the most likely place for the MK after high school graduation is college. Plus they want to be sure that the kids are not short changed in their education on the field, so kids are constantly encouraged to do well and participate in everything in order to compete successfully in college.

(d) Small mission school classes and specialized instruction add pressure to succeed.

(e) Bible verse:

"Whatever you do, work at it with all your heart, as working for the Lord, not for human masters," Colossians 3:23 NIV

Complications

(a) When an MK lives on a small mission center or compound he can quite easily be the best in something he is good at. When he arrives in the U.S. he suddenly finds he has a whole nation to compete with. In areas appropriate to the U.S. culture, he can no longer be the best. In areas which are not appropriate to the U.S., his skill is not appreciated. In light of this and all the other ethical conflicts, many MKs begin to feel that they are not capable of doing anything right. Since being able to do things well is their very definition of success, this can make them feel like total failures.

(b) Many MKs can spend large amounts of time going after a goal which has no other conceivable gain; six months on a hiking or bike tour; a month building an art project;

the mastery of an unusual foreign language.

Success (Self Worth) Is Adjusting To A New Situation

States-side opposite: Adjusting to a new situation, is a valuable achievement, like learning a new skill. If one fails to adjust to, say a new state, there is a certain amount of freedom to decide to move back home. Also, it would suffice to most Americans to have adjusted on the surface.

Explanation of MK value

(a) For generations it has been difficult for missionaries to adjust to the field. Only those who "stuck it out" against tremendous odds are able to complete the work. Thus, for the missionary a good adjustment to a difficult environment is a key to success and this value is passed on.

(b) Because so many MKs in the past have had difficulty adjusting to the U.S., there is a tremendous pressure put on by parents and others not to have difficulty. The MK knows they have done all they can to make things as comfortable for him as possible and the rest is up to him. He does not want to let them down.

(c) Throughout their life most MKs must adjust to new situations many times over. They learn very early that the key to peace and happiness is to adjust as quickly as possible and this becomes a major key to success in life in their view.

Possible Complications

(a) The most significant complication this value presents is the MK's reaction to his adjustment to the United States. There are many areas in which an MK never will fit into the mold of the average States-sider. To a certain extent he may never fully adjust. If he expects to have adjusted well by a certain period of time (such as 2-3 years) and finds that he is still struggling after 5-10 years, he may consider himself to be a complete failure.

(b) Because admitting to not adjusting well is admitting major life failure, many MKs lack the courage to tell anyone that they need help, or even to admit that they are homesick. Sometimes, due to this factor alone, they may wait until it is too late to get help with this perspective.

(c) Pressure to adjust well forces MKs to do things well, which will help them fit in, even though those things go against their conscience. They then live with ongoing guilt and feel like failures in other areas.

(d) Shame caused by not adjusting well prevents people from gaining an accurate picture of how many MKs are having trouble adjusting to the United States. Most MKs would never admit failure in this area to themselves or their immediate families, let alone on a questionnaire.

Comments:

Most of all everyone needs to realize that it may take far more time to adjust to the United States than one might expect. It might not be possible at all if it were not for the fact that the U.S. is a "melting pot" of cultures. In fact, adjustment beyond what is specifically practical, including whatever is necessary to get along with others and to be content in his necessary work, may be a waste of effort and may not necessary at all. For example, a person who moves to the north is still expected to have a southern accent and southern tastes years after he has moved. MKs who intend to go back to the field should be allowed to do so without ever really adjusting to the United States except to the extent that is necessary to get support and to get along with the other missionaries. MKs who simply do not possess the skills they need to make a complete cultural adjustment ought to be allowed to feel content with a job in the culture where they feel most comfortable.

RELIGION AND POLITICS

Political Views on Foreign Issues Are Usually Different Than Their States-side Friends' Due to Experience Overseas

States-side opposite; States-siders can only base their political opinions about the outside world on what they read or are told.

Explanation of MK value

(a) Life overseas and exposure to other forms of government, other cultures, other beliefs, and other lifestyles.
(b) News in the U.S. is actually quite limited as much of it is sensation oriented and does not create a whole picture.

Possible Complications

(a) States-siders might be disgusted at finding an MK who seems to be such a mature Christian but believes so differently about such basic issues as Capitalism and Socialism.
(b) MKs might be disgusted at ideas in States-siders they ought to respect, (such as church leaders or grandparents), which appear to them to be so one-sided and naive.

[207]

Money In Religion Is Resented (Offering Pleas, Fund Drives Etc.)

Explanation of MK value

(a) On some mission fields churches never do much about offering unless it is to take up a collection for a specific cause.

(b) Missionaries are on the receiving end of the support system and not on the giving end. Children do not see that their parents are getting these funds because it is all done behind the scenes through accounts and not by bringing home paychecks.

(c) The nature of many pleas sounds unBiblical to MKs. Missionaries teach their children that we depend on God, not man for our provision. Many pleas make it clear that the receiver is depending on the audience to whom he is speaking.

Possible Complications

(a) Many MKs have left churches because of their regular offering appeals. (States-siders do this too, but to a lesser degree.)

(b) A Godly Pastor may be viewed as unGodly, or hypocritical because of his pleas for money, and be ignored or resented.

FRIENDS

Friendships Are More Important Than Any Other Thing

States-side opposite: Friendships are important but not as

important as money, lifestyle, jobs, family and hobbies.

Explanation of MK value

(a) On the field there are not many things in a person's life and even families may come and go, but friendships last through everything.

(b) Parents teach from the Bible that relationships are more important than any other thing. They also show this by giving their lives to bring others into a relationship with Christ.

Possible Complications

(a) MKs may be offended when "friends" put work, or time with relatives, or sports ahead of them.

(b) MKs may put friendships ahead of their jobs and get fired.

All Friendships Are To Be Very Deep

States-sider opposites; All kinds of relationships are valid, whatever they happen to be like. No effort is made to make most relationships deep or meaningful. Such a relationship if it develops, is seen as a rare and valuable occurrence. Relationships are expected to be surface friendships with a few exceptions.

Explanation of MK value

(a) When children must be away from families, they naturally try to replace those necessary close human relationships with friends.

(b) If the MKs have grown up with the same few peers. Those peers will have been the one steady factor in their lives.

Often peers move on to boarding school together, when even families are left behind. They become close naturally, and eventually the MK gets used to having such relationships as though they were the norm.

(c) Living in a small town with everything in common, tends to produce very close friends, as most things are mutually experienced.

Possible Complications

(a) One common complaint by States-siders, especially when dating, is that the MK is "trying too hard". Often, they are trying to make the relationship grow faster than what the States-sider would be prepared for.

(b) In an attempt to foster deep relationships, MKs often make themselves very vulnerable by sharing personal issues with others who have no intention of understanding. It is virtually incomprehensible to some MKs that some people would have no intention of understanding everything about their friends.

(c) A long-term relationship that remains casual, for example with relatives, may be a source of frustration to an MK, who may wonder what went wrong.

(d) States-siders may be offended by the MKs "advances" before they have built a sufficient level of trust which takes time.

Comment

MKs should try to enjoy and express friendships in a more shallow way than they may be accustomed to, even with people they love very much. They can manage by sharing certain

[210]

things with some and other things with other people and having lots of casual friends.

States-siders do love to have a few deep friendships so with patience, these can be developed.

Dropping In Is Expected

Explanation of MK value

(a) In many locations overseas telephones are either non-existent or expensive, and distances close, making it much more convenient to drop by a friend's house than to call ahead. This situation is accommodated by several more factors:

People expect others to drop in on them, so they remain somewhat prepared for this at all times.

People do not demand as much when they drop by knowing that they came uninvited. For example, one might feel free to finish up the work in the garden with the friend looking on or pitching in rather than finding it necessary to stop immediately, apologize, clean-up, and produce a beverage.

People become more aware of each other's personal habits and are less likely to interfere with these inadvertently. For example, in a short time one would learn that Beverly likes to take a nap on Sundays, but Susan loves company. Or that the Smiths eat at six PM while the Johnsons eat at eight.

(b) In MK culture friendships are more important than time or almost anything else, so if a friend arrives at a bad time, the MK is quick to accommodate him changing his schedule accordingly.

(c) Calling ahead in small town or other foreign settings is often a sign of formality, indicating that preparation or other accommodation is expected at the meeting.

Possible Complications

(a) States-siders may be offended by MKs (and missionaries) dropping by to visit without calling ahead.

(b) States-siders may be seriously offended by MKs dropping by frequently, especially if they stay around each time without stopping to think about what their hosts may have been doing before they arrived. They may assume that it was the hosts responsibility to either accommodate them or inform them of their other plans.

(c) MKs may drop by the home of someone whom they do not know, but whom they would like to get to know, thereby creating the first impression that they are "strange" and diminishing the possibility of future friendship, which was the very thing they tried to create.

(d) MKs may feel offended and left out when no one comes to visit them. They may feel that they have offended people or simply that no one cares for their company.

(e) MKs may not call to invite people over or call to visit someone feeling that to do so would demand formality, and that they may not be able to be prepared, nor would they want their friends to have to get ready for them. This will cause a lot of frustration for the MK whose values place friendships higher than other activities. "Why should I not be able to visit with my friends just because neither of us have the time to entertain, to keep the house ready for guests or to provide refreshments?"

Comment

This cross-cultural conflict can be the source of much loneliness, depression and sense of failure for MKs as patterns are created which prevent them from maintaining relationships with others.

Accept Anyone And Everyone As A Potential Friend

Because everyone is accepted, serious relationships can begin in a wide variety of circumstances.

States-side opposite; States-siders generally do not expect anyone to be a friend, unless time has allowed them to get to know each other. Care is taught by parents regarding dating other races, other nationalities, and especially other economic brackets. The main concern is other values. People tend to gather with people like themselves.

Explanation of MK value

(a) On the field missionaries' work requires them to be friendly towards all kinds of heathen people, and poor starving people, and people of many faiths and nationalities. If an MK is living at the site of the ministry, not in a center or boarding school, he or she may have to choose childhood friends from among such people. Parents would not teach caution in such instances since the local children would not present any type of danger. Certainly, passing on any prejudices would be inappropriate.

(b) MKs who must move around frequently must learn to

make friends quickly.

(c) In the safety of centers and dorms they need never worry about the type of characters they are likely to run into. Anyone willing to be a friend is okay, and the sooner friends are made, the better. By the end of the year they may have to move again.

Possible Complications

(a) MKs may be friendly with all kinds of people, to the consternation of caring people around them. This might get them in trouble or it might make them good Samaritans. For example, in college, Muslims, Hindus, drug addicts, Atheists and mediums would not be exempt from their open extended hand of friendship.

(b) MKs may get involved in what most States-siders would call the wrong crowd, and finding that they are unconditionally accepted there, unlike at church, become drawn away from Christianity.

(c) MKs may open up to people, especially relatives and church members, right away upon meeting them, making themselves vulnerable to back biting, gossip, or disappointing responses.

(d) The worst thing I have frequently seen come out of this is seriously crippling romantic partnerships. The couple starts out as "just friends" with someone they know is of dubious morals or beliefs. Before they know it they are romantically involved and finally hopelessly in love. These relationships become a trap and many MKs have been brought to the point of despair by close dependency on ("yoking with") a person who has no solutions to the many problems MKs face, but only added their own problems. The only way out is through devastating heartbreak. These couples are often closer and thus more heartbroken than most because of the hardships and social persecution they have faced together. Staying together often creates years of unstable and unhappy marriages sometimes ending in divorce. Usually the MK has started out feeling that he or she was going to minister to the partner, but ministry seldom wins against chemistry.

Comments

States-siders come across thousands of people in their lives. With many of these, close relationships could negatively affect you, and they don't know which are which. People could be politically offended and impact your work or your families. Some evil people could actually harm you. There are other people with whom you simply don't have enough hours in the day to maintain a close relationship. Nevertheless, there are a few people which one can learn to trust and do life with.

Developed and Fostered Relationships Are More Important Than Automatic Ones Such As Family

States-side opposite: Fulfill your obligations to your relatives first, and then oblige your friends if there is time left over.

Explanation of MK value

(a) On the field there are no relatives so there are no opportunities to pay them special attention. Other missionaries are often called aunt and uncle, further confusing things.

(b) Some MKs grow up in boarding schools where their peers become their family, making them of almost equal value growing up.

(c) Most MKs are prepared from an early age for semi-permanent separation from parents after high school or even earlier. By the time this actually happens the message is clear; focus on the relationships around you, not on ones which are by blood. MKs have few automatic relationships until they move to the U.S. as adults, by which time they and their relatives hardly know each other.

(d) Many MKs find it harder to get along with their own relatives than with other States-siders since their own relatives expect more cultural compliance. This emphasizes the MKs impression that relationships can't be automatic.

Possible Complications

(a) MKs may make no effort to get to know relatives per se, and may only develop relationships with those relatives who have made a specific effort to get to know them.

(b) MKs may offend their relatives by choosing to attend an outing with peers rather than a family dinner or even reunion.

(c) MKs may misunderstand a relative's efforts to get to know them; a young man may wonder why his single aunt in her forties has invited him to dinner.

(d) MKs may react the opposite and expect much too much of relatives, perhaps due to memories of doting grandparents on furloughs. Or, they expect relatives to act like their MK friends or their parents' fellow missionaries. Given that their culture is different in various values, this may give the relatives the impression that they are trying to take advantage of them.

Comment

The fact that an MK has a wonderful relationship with one or more of his relatives does not in any way determine that he does not still hold relationships with friends above those with family. He may simply have accepted those particular relatives into his circle of friends!

DIALOGUES, SELF EXPRESSION

Honesty-To Extreme

Explanation of MK value

(a) In a small group, dishonesty is bound to be exposed sooner or later. It is better just to tell the truth from the start. Example; In the city if a friend asks you how you are doing, when you have been sick, you might say "fine" preferring not to get them involved. However, in a very small group, if a friend asked you how you were, and you said "fine", and then they dropped by, or you got worse, and they heard, they might wonder why you had not been open with them.

(b) Honesty is explicitly taught by Christians. In the U.S. this is tempered with TV and business ethics which allow for a wide definition of "honesty," while on the field it is taken quite literally.

[217]

Possible Complications

MKs may share information about themselves which puts them in a bad light. Because the States-side boss assumes he or she is only looking at the tip of the iceberg when it comes to exposed problems, he will interpret the shared problem to be far worse than it is. This is a very common problem with job interviews but also occurs long after jobs are secured. Most States-siders will go out of their way to avoid sharing information which might possibly be misunderstood.

White lies are such a well-known part of States-side daily life that a high proportion of TV sitcoms are devoted to just that: Trying to get around telling somebody something which is "none of their business." MKs would instead, expect the boss to expect the best of them. Unfortunately, that is not the usual pattern for bosses who can easily find another employee which they have no suspicions about. Trust in a relationship is extremely important to an MK. Some MKs would rather not even work for someone who they think might not trust them no matter what.

RECREATION

Loss Of Freedom Is Resented—Rules Applying To Nature Sports Are Resented

States-side opposite: Rules concerning the outdoors are respected and appreciated as an insurance of safety. Most rules are to protect the environment. Some are to protect the parks from getting sued for any accidents.

Urban States-siders will find it difficult to imagine why the United States means "loss of freedom for recreation". Yet

[218]

many environments in the world provide readily available recreation without any restrictions.

Explanation of MK value

On some fields, there are few rules, if any, about the environment except in villages themselves. Many MKs are used to being able to hike, hunt, or explore, for as far as they are able without restrictions of any kind. People in this type of situation often become accustomed to relieving tension and stress and to dealing with adversity by getting away where "all is fair and belongs to God alone" to sort things out for a while. The fact that in the U.S. nothing belongs to God alone, but all of it belongs to people or the government or companies etc. can be a real source of frustration. It must be difficult to imagine the extent of this frustration if one has never tasted this level of freedom before. It is not the lack of recreation itself so much as the idea that one cannot get away to anywhere that belongs to "no one".

Even in countries where everything is owned by someone, rules in parks and recreation areas are not usually as restrictive.

Possible Complications

(a) MKs may feel like prisoners and further resent life in the U.S., especially if it was not their choice to come here.

(b) National parks and recreation areas may never be appreciated or even used if the park rules and regulations make the MK, who is going to the wilderness to get away from human society, feel that he has never gotten away. He may feel like he can never find a place to really let go and rest.

[219]

(c) MKs may not understand the rules in parks and may subconsciously see them as an affront to human intelligence. "Why can't we go off the main trail? Do they really think we would get lost?"

<u>Tips For MKs</u>

Most of the rules in parks are for the safety of the park, rather than to control the actions of the people. The word "park" indicates a concerted effort to protect the environment. This may be true even when a guide claims it is for safety.

An MK who really feels the need for more freedom than what is granted the American public should make the effort to get involved in wilderness activities on a professional level where much more freedom is granted. The key is to accept being treated as an amateur until you have proven yourself as a pro. Licenses to most wilderness areas can be obtained.

Watching Sports Is Looked Down On

<u>Explanation of MK value</u>

(a) Many MKs have never seen an adult whose lifestyle they respect, watching TV sports. Few missionaries can do this on the field. By the time they return to the U.S. for furlough they are so out of what is going on that they often have lost interest.

(b) Some MKs are not familiar enough with the way sports appears on TV to follow them without considerable strain. Following TV sports is a skill which is acquired over time by States-siders while they grow up.

(c) When there is no enjoyment in the watching, no concern over who wins, and little or no social interaction between those who watch, then sports remains as a time-consuming, non-constructive activity, and this is the view held by most MKs.

(d) In other countries a different set of sports is often played, such as soccer or cricket.

Possible Complications

(a) MKs may be offended when they are invited to someone's home and the host proceeds to occupy his time by watching competitive sports on TV. The MK experiences this in the exact same way as one would if one were invited to a person's home to visit and the host spent the time reading his favorite novel.

(b) If the MK is not actually offended, he will at least be bored and may try to avoid the company of that person in the future. This would include relatives who did this at a family reunion.

HOME

Home Is On The Field Or No Particular Place At All

Sates-side: This is not opposite. Home is really wherever one's childhood is.

Explanation of MK value

Growing up on the field is the one and only source of this value. Wherever one spends the most time, automatically becomes home, with childhood time counting as double or much more. Many missions and missionaries make the mistake of trying keep the field country from becoming home to the children. This is impossible, and only makes for maladjusted persons. The sounds we wake up to, the smells, the conversations, the activities we do, and the steps we take all day; all that we are accustomed to is how we imagine home. No amount of teaching to the contrary can make us understand that the sights and sounds and smells of a crisp Saturday morning in the middle of summer vacation with all the promise and security of fun things we have invented to do with our childhood friends, are "nothing compared with the country that mommy and daddy grew up in." If an MK has spent his entire childhood on the field, that field will be home, even if it must exist only in his imagination.

Possible Complications

(a) The move to the United States is far more devastating for an MK who has grown up on the field, than for one who has merely spent a short time on a field. It is in fact an exile, causing the same level of stress as would permanent exile to a foreign country for an American.

(b) Often missions demand that MKs settle down and adjust to America before allowing them to return to the field as missionaries. This makes about as much sense as it would to say to an American missionary to the Inuit, that he must first be completely adjusted to Africa before he can move to Alaska.

(c) If the MK has spent his entire life on the field one can assume that homesickness for more than just family will play a major part in his adjustment to the United States.

It Is Dishonorable And A Failure To Be Homesick

Explanation of MK value

(a) Homesickness exemplifies failure in the most basic sense for MKs due to their basic definition of success in part being "to be able to adjust well."

(b) Homesickness in the boarding situations is often countered with the idea that "You don't want your parents to have to quit their work, do you?" It is often made fun of.

Possible Complications

(a) Because Adult MKs seldom express homesickness, it can be easily overlooked that an underlying problem they may be facing is just that.

(b) Because it is "shameful" to admit homesickness, MKs who are severely homesick may not express it and get help before it becomes overwhelming. Often there are relatives or family who if they really knew the severity of the homesickness which the MK is facing might be more than willing to help out towards a visit home. However, even when asked, the MK will often not admit that this is his problem.

(c) Because homesickness is seen as failure rather than as suffering, a natural grieving process is hindered or prevented.

There are many more examples of differences in culture, but this will give one enough of an idea to apply the principles to his or her own situation.

IMPORTANT: There is a much more exhausting list of MK values and ethics available for free as a simple PDF file. Over 100 pages of such culture clashes have been compiled by the author of this book and her friends and can be ordered at:

edierainforest@yahoo.com

The list is in raw form and will not be sold in a professional format but could be extremely helpful for a struggling adult MK and/or his family.

FROM THE AUTHOR

I wrote the core of this book in the mid-1980s. It has been completely updated recently and I still stand by it. After I wrote the original version, I got an opportunity to work for the *National Geographic Society* leading two expeditions to my home country of Papua New Guinea. I wrote an article for their magazine in February of 1994 called "Return to Hunstein Forest." In the process, I was a catalyst for saving the rainforest I loved as a child. I published a book later in 2012 called **Rendezvous with a Rainforest** about those adventures.

Shortly after the expeditions, a particularly extreme family tragedy struck me in a very personal way and I became mentally ill for the next 20 years. My book **Crocodile Set Free:** *a Christian Mental Health Mystery* is a memoir of those years and was published in 2014. This book covers many aspects of mental illness caused by Christianity as well as by boarding schools and other issues.

Yours, Sincerely

Edie Bakker

Also by Edie Bakker

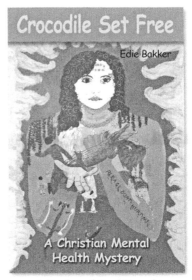

Pure Adventure!

A rainforest in Papua New Guinea is being threatened by logging! Edie gets the attention of the National Geographic Society and through two NGS expeditions and a *National Geographic Magazine* article she realizes the only way to save the rainforest is through a relationship with the forest landowners. This book is filled with adventure as they attempt to climb unreached Mt. Hunstein and strive to save the pristine virgin rainforest with its magnificent trees, clear rivers and Birds of Paradise.

Will they, or won't they save the rainforest?

A Profound Soul Search!

A shocking personal tragedy occurs, and Edie's world is destroyed. Deep searching as well as counseling also uncovers memories of foster homes and spiritual/emotional abuse. Overcome by it all, she gradually descends into insanity. To get well, she must challenge Christianity head on. She tears apart her belief system and looks for true agape love.

Will she recover her faith and sanity?

Both books are available on Amazon.com.

Made in the USA
Monee, IL
22 November 2019